THE SCHOOLS HISTORY PROJECT
· OFFICIAL TEXT ·
S·H·P

CORE TEXTS
FOR GCSE

THE STRUGGLE FOR PEACE IN
NORTHERN
IRELAND

a modern world study

Ben Walsh

Series Editors:
Christopher Culpin
Ian Dawson

JOHN MURRAY

The Schools History Project

This project was set up by the Schools Council in 1972. Its main aim was to suggest suitable aims for history teachers, and to promote the use of appropriate materials and teaching methods for their realisation. This involved a reconsideration of the nature of history and its relevance in secondary schools, the design of a syllabus framework which shows the uses of history in the education of adolescents, and the setting up of appropriate examinations.

Since 1978 the project has been based at Trinity and All Saints' College, Leeds. It is now self-funding and with the advent of the National Curriculum it has expanded its publications to provide courses for Key Stage 3, and for a range of GCSE and A level syllabuses. The project provides INSET for all aspects of National Curriculum, GCSE and A level history. The SHP website can be found at www.tasc.ac.uk/shp

Series consultant
Terry Fiehn

Note: the wording and sentence structure of some written sources have been adapted and simplified to make them accessible to all students, while faithfully preserving the sense of the original.

Words printed in SMALL CAPITALS are defined in the Glossary on page 138.

Acknowledgements

The author would like to express appreciation and thanks to the following people who have provided invaluable help and advice through the writing and editing of this book: Dr Roger Austin of the University of Ulster in Coleraine; Professor Patrick Buckland, formerly of the Institute of Irish Studies at the University of Liverpool and now a Trustee of the Warrington Project; Sheelagh Dean, History Adviser with the South Eastern Education and Library Board in Northern Ireland; Carmel Gallagher, Assistant Director (Curriculum and Assessment) for the Council for Curriculum, Examinations and Assessment in Northern Ireland; Michael Hall, Community Think Tanks Co-ordinator in Northern Ireland; Vivien Kelly, History Inspector with the Southern Education and Library Board in Northern Ireland; Yvonne Murphy, Librarian at the Political Collection of the Linen Hall Library in Belfast; Heather Thompson, History Adviser with the North Eastern Education and Library Board in Northern Ireland.

The author would also like to thank the many teachers and students who have tried out and commented upon various sections of the book at different stages, including his own students at Stafford College. Finally, many thanks must also go to Barbara Kotara for typing the manuscript.

First published in 2000
by John Murray (Publishers) Ltd
50 Albemarle Street
London W1S 4BD

Reprinted 2001

Layouts by Eric Drewery
Artwork by Art Construction, Linden Artists, Tony Randell
Typeset in 10½/12 pt Walbaum Book by Wearset, Boldon, Tyne and Wear
Colour separations by Colourscript, Mildenhall, Suffolk
Printed and bound by G. Canale, Italy

A catalogue entry for this title is available from the British Library.

ISBN 0 7195 7472 2
Teachers' Resource Book ISBN 0 7195 7473 0

Contents

● ●

Northern Ireland as a Modern World Study

THE CONFLICT IN Northern Ireland is a challenging and rewarding Modern World Study.

Relevant history

Northern Ireland is a regular item on the television or radio news, and in the newspapers, but few people feel they truly understand events there. A Modern World Study of Northern Ireland can help you see these unfolding events in their historical context.

Contemporary history

The main focus of the study is on the period after 1969. This contemporary history is therefore part of the oral history of many individuals, families and communities both in mainland Britain and on either side of the border between Northern Ireland and the Republic of Ireland.

Significant history

Studying Northern Ireland's history raises issues about how democratic governments respond to the expressed wishes of their own people and how citizens of a democratic state should seek to change things they disagree with. It also highlights the problems involved in balancing the rights of different groups in society.

Mythical history

People involved in the Northern Ireland conflict see the same historical events in different ways. Some people use their interpretation of history to justify extreme views or actions. This topic exposes you to the power of myth and to the task of the historian in disentangling 'myth' from reality.

International history

Northern Ireland's history is not just an Irish story. It is also a British story, a European story and a world story. All over the world, especially in the USA and Canada, there are people whose ancestors came from both Northern Ireland and the Republic. At different times these people have played their part in resolving or heightening conflict. More recently, the European Union has tried to play its part in the struggle for peace in Northern Ireland. This topic demonstrates both the strengths and the weaknesses of 'outsiders' in helping to solve a country's problems.

Ongoing history

Much of the history you have studied may feel dead and buried. This is not. Something may happen tomorrow to make this book completely out of date; then it is over to you, as a historian, to seek to understand it.

1 *GET YOUR BEARINGS*

> 66 *In Northern Ireland, our [programmes] are all about normal life. More than 80 per cent of Radio Ulster's output is concerned with normality.* 99

> 66 *Then the shooting started. I heard a man screaming, 'I have been shot!' The shooting was still going on and on. Then my mammy and aunt ran out into the shooting.* 99

Impressions of Northern Ireland

DO YOU THINK of Northern Ireland as a beautiful place, with magnificent mountains, rivers and lakes? Do you think of its people as friendly, hospitable and generous, with a great sense of humour? Or do you think of it as a place of violence, conflict and prejudice, as it is often shown in the media?

In this course you will study the violent conflict that erupted in 1969 and continued until the end of the 1990s. We call it 'the TROUBLES'. However, while violence has been a fact of life in Northern Ireland for the past 30 years, many normal things happen too. While the impression that Northern Ireland is a violent place is not wrong, it is not the whole story.

Ignorance matters!

Throughout this book, you will discover that ignorance matters. Ignorance has played an important part in causing conflict in Ireland. For example, for much of the twentieth century the NATIONALIST and UNIONIST communities of Northern Ireland lived apart, almost totally SEGREGATED. Nationalists and Unionists hardly met.

The result was that by the 1960s there was an amazing level of ignorance in each community about their neighbours. Unionist and nationalist communities failed to understand each other's hopes and intentions. The gap was filled by lies, rumours, half truths and misunderstandings. Ignorance breeds fear. Fear breeds violence.

Prods have no sense of humour.

Catholics' eyes are closer together.

Equally damaging is the ignorance of outsiders. Throughout the Northern Ireland conflict the people and government of the United Kingdom could do little to help bring peace, because they knew practically nothing about Northern Ireland and many of them did not care, either. At many times the issue of Northern Ireland was only a sideshow, a distraction from political affairs in London.

■ SOURCE INVESTIGATION

You will learn a little bit about Northern Ireland from the following sources. You will probably learn a good deal more about your own knowledge of Northern Ireland (or lack of it!).

1. Think hard about your impressions of Northern Ireland and the Troubles. Summarise your impressions in a list of words or short phrases.
2. Look at Sources 1–6 and their captions. These give some varied impressions of Northern Ireland and the Troubles. Decide which sources fit with your mental image of Northern Ireland and which ones do not.
3. From the evidence in **only these sources**, how accurate was your original image? Explain this.
4. You have to find four sources to be used in a pamphlet, which is to be called *Northern Ireland for the Ignorant*. Choose them from Sources 1–6 and explain your choices.

SOURCE 1 A mural from a nationalist area of Belfast showing burnt-out Catholic housing and women banging bin lids on the ground. At the height of the Troubles, they used to bang bin lids on the floor to warn that army or police patrols were approaching nationalist areas

SOURCE 2 A small boy getting closer than usual to a British Army soldier on patrol in Northern Ireland. This photograph was taken soon after the IRA ceasefire of August 1994, which lasted until February 1996

SOURCE 3 A photograph taken in August 1998 showing the aftermath of a bomb in Omagh, County Tyrone. The bomb was planted by a REPUBLICAN group opposed to the peace process, and killed 29 people

SOURCE 4 A peace rally at the People's Park, Ballymena, in October 1976

SOURCE 5 A diary entry written by eleven-year-old Bridie Murphy in 1994, describing her experience of the Troubles

Then, later that night, my Aunt Lorraine and Mammy were worried because my oldest sister had not come home and it was getting late. Mammy had seen men on the Protestant side of the fence. They were cutting through the fence. Every time that happened before, the Protestant men came over and shot one of us Catholics. My mammy rang the police and told them what she had seen and they told her not to worry, they would make sure nothing happened, but she was still worried.

Then, about a quarter past eleven that night, my sister came home. She was talking to a young fella who was a passenger in the taxi. My aunt called to her to hurry in. They were in the hall and my mammy was telling my sister off for not coming in early. Then the shooting started. I heard a man screaming, 'I have been shot!' The shooting was still going on and on. Then my mammy and aunt ran out into the shooting.

SOURCE 6 A senior BBC journalist speaking at a lecture in 1977 about what was covered on radio and TV in Northern Ireland

In Northern Ireland, our extensive coverage of sport, our sponsorship of musicians, writers and actors, the daily advertising of events and discussion of household matters in regional programmes, such as Good Morning Ulster [and] Taste of Hunni, and our access and community programmes are all about normal life. More than 80 per cent of Radio Ulster's output is concerned with normality.

Navigating Northern Ireland politics: who thinks what?

DURING THIS COURSE you will discover that there are many different political parties in Northern Ireland. One of the hardest yet most important parts of navigating your way through the course is working out an overall map of where these parties stand. Which groups and individuals are on which side? What do they believe in?

You will find that some groups appear to be closely linked to each other, but then turn out to have very different ideas.

The information panels below give you a brief introduction to the main nationalist groups and the main unionist groups.

Nationalists

- Nationalists are generally Catholic.

- They see themselves as Irish rather than British.

- Nationalists see the island of Ireland as one place, and generally want it united as one state. However, not all Nationalists want exactly the same thing.
  a) At different times in Northern Ireland's history many moderate Nationalists have preferred to remain part of the UK.
  b) Democratic Nationalists have also campaigned for equal rights for the nationalist community within Northern Ireland: housing, job opportunities, etc.
  c) At the other end of the nationalist spectrum are hardline Republicans. They want separation from the UK and the creation of a united Ireland.

- The main nationalist parties are the SDLP (Social and Democratic Labour Party) and SINN FEIN (pronounced Shin Fayn). Not all Nationalists agree about how their aims should be achieved.
  a) The SDLP is totally committed to democratic, peaceful methods.
  b) Sinn Fein, although a political party, is closely associated with the IRA (Irish Republican Army).

- The IRA and INLA are the main republican PARAMILITARIES who use violence to achieve their aims. To Republicans, they are freedom fighters. To their opponents, they are terrorists and criminal thugs.

- Another important organisation is the Ancient Order of Hibernians, a Catholic community and social organisation which organises parades and does charitable work.

- Buzzwords: Ireland; Irish; Republic; GAELIC words such as *Saoirse* (freedom); Gaelic or Catholic names such as Padraig or Bernadette; the rebellion of 1798 and Wolfe Tone (one of its leading figures).

Unionists

Unionists have nothing to do with trade unions. Nor do they want anything to do with a 'united Ireland'. The Union they stand for is the union between Northern Ireland and Britain.

Like the Nationalists, the Unionists come in different shades.

- Unionists are generally Protestant. (It is important to remember that there are several different types of Protestant. The two largest groups are Anglicans and Presbyterians, but there are others as well.)
  a) They believe that union with Great Britain is good for Northern Ireland economically.
  b) Some believe that if there was a united Ireland, Protestants would be discriminated against.
  c) They are generally stronger in the north and east of Northern Ireland, especially in Belfast.

- The Unionists are also called LOYALISTS (i.e. loyal to Britain), though this usually refers to more extreme Unionists.

- The ULSTER UNIONIST PARTY is the main party representing unionist views. It is totally committed to peaceful democratic methods. It is the biggest single party in Northern Ireland.

- The Democratic Unionist Party (DUP) is a more hardline political party.

- The main paramilitary groups are the Ulster Defence Association (UDA) and the Ulster Volunteer Force (UVF). There are many splinter groups, such as the Ulster Freedom Fighters (UFF). They use violence to achieve their aims.

- Another important group is the LOYAL ORANGE ORDER, a Protestant organisation organised into lodges (branches). It is best known for its marches in the summer months, but also does charitable and community work. Critics say it has too much political influence in Northern Ireland.

- Buzzwords: ULSTER; Union; Loyalist; British; William of Orange ('King Billy'); 1690 and the Battle of the Boyne.

■ TASK

This graph is a way of classifying the various groups in Northern Ireland that you will come across in this book. It classifies groups by their aims (whether or not they want Northern Ireland to stay part of the UK) and their methods (whether they use violence or democracy to achieve their aims).

Make a start by placing the following groups on the graph. The further along the arms you put an organisation, the more extreme it is.

■ The IRA is already shown. It is positioned there because it holds republican (extreme nationalist) views and it has used violence to achieve its aims.
■ Ulster Unionist Party: a democratic party in favour of the Union between Northern Ireland and Britain. It is opposed to violence.
■ Ulster Volunteer Force: a loyalist (extreme unionist) paramilitary organisation. It is completely opposed to the idea of a united Ireland and has used violence to achieve its aims.
■ SDLP: the main nationalist party. It is totally opposed to violence. It wants to achieve a united Ireland by peaceful means.

The idea is to use this graph again and again. As you come across other groups in your studies, place them on this graph. You could also put key individuals there as well – try someone who is currently in the news. It is a good idea to use a pencil in case you change your mind or in case any groups or individuals change their policies.

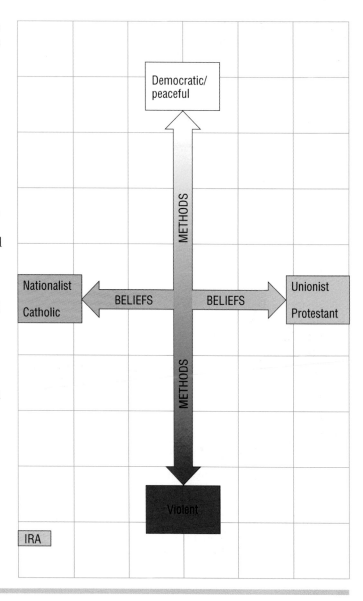

The Third Way

■ A substantial number of people in Northern Ireland do not see themselves as either Unionist or Nationalist.
■ In the 1991 Northern Ireland census, 7.3 per cent of people refused to put any entry on the part of the form which asked about religion.
■ Many people in Northern Ireland do not vote for the traditional parties. Some do not vote at all, others vote for the Alliance Party.
■ The Alliance Party is a moderate unionist party which actively tries to gain support from all sections of the Northern Ireland communities.
■ Northern Ireland also has a small but growing immigrant community, such as the Chinese community in Belfast. They are rarely involved in unionist or nationalist issues.

Terminology: the same but different!

The different communities in Northern Ireland have different names for their country, their towns and the events that have shaped their history. For example, some nationalist communities would not use the term 'Northern Ireland'. They would prefer 'the North', 'the Six Counties', 'Ulster' (though this last term refers to nine counties).

What is the conflict in Northern Ireland all about?

MOST PEOPLE AGREE that the conflict in Northern Ireland is complicated and tragic. But what is it about? As you can see, there are plenty of possible answers.

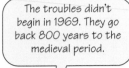
The troubles didn't begin in 1969. They go back 800 years to the medieval period.

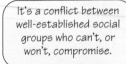
It's a conflict between well-established social groups who can't, or won't, compromise.

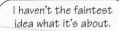
I haven't the faintest idea what it's about.

It's a political issue about who controls Northern Ireland.

It's all about religion – Catholic versus Protestant.

It's a conflict between different nations – Ireland and Britain.

It's about money. It's about who owns the land and the business and who gets the money.

As these remarks show, there are plenty of different opinions. Do not worry if you are not clear what the conflict is all about. Even leading experts in Northern Ireland, the Republic, Britain, the USA and just about everywhere else cannot come up with a simple answer.

Sources 1–6 (perhaps they should really be called 'opinions 1–6') give some idea of the range of views.

■ TASK

Here is a series of statements about the situation in Northern Ireland.

- The conflict is a political struggle for power in Northern Ireland.
- The conflict in Northern Ireland is a religious struggle.
- The conflict in Northern Ireland is a political struggle which looks like a religious one.
- The conflict in Northern Ireland is a religious struggle which looks like a political one.
- The conflict in Northern Ireland is a struggle between two nationalities (Irish and British).

Some of the statements are supported by Sources 1–6 and some are not.

In small groups, decide

a) which statements are supported by Sources 1–6
b) which statements you do not accept as accurate
c) which statements you do accept as accurate.

If you accept none of these statements as accurate write your own statement about what the conflict is about.

Explain your choices by referring to the information and sources on page 9.

*"Oh dear, not the **Irish** Christians again!"*

SOURCE 2 James O'Connell, Department of Peace Studies, University of Bradford

66 *If this Irish conflict is not about religion, it is organised around Christian groups, and it is made worse by religious bitterness. It is really a struggle for political power; and it is fed by the fears of two minority groups, one a minority in Ireland and the other a minority in Northern Ireland.* 99

SOURCE 3 Historian A.T.Q. Stewart, formerly a leading Northern Ireland academic historian at Queen's University, Belfast

66 *The exact cause of the quarrel, or its survival, is often obscure to the onlooker. In many countries it is assumed that it is a holy war. The fact is, however, that the quarrel is not about religion. It is stubbornly a constitutional problem ... the conflict in Ulster is about political power and who should wield it.* 99

SOURCE 4 Roy Gillespie, DUP Councillor for Ballymena, speaking at the DUP conference in 1991. The DUP is Ian Paisley's party, and is strongly Unionist

66 *The Roman Catholic Church is the problem in our province ... Rome's aim is to destroy Protestantism, our children, our children's children, our way of life and the Bible.* 99

SOURCE 5 Stephen Mitchel, a Protestant preacher, interviewed for the BBC 2 programme *Leviathan* in 1998

66 *There are many Protestants in Northern Ireland today who proudly claim to be Protestant, but never darken the doors of a church. They would never come to God's house to be guided by the scriptures they so strongly claim to defend ... Protestantism is a political identity now, more than a spiritual one. In fact many Protestant politicians would openly admit to being atheist.* 99

SOURCE 6 Political scientist Jurg Steiner commenting on Northern Ireland in his book *European Democracies*, published in 1995

66 *In Northern Ireland, the problem appears on the surface to be a religious one, and the mass media usually speak of civil strife between Protestants and Catholics. But, below the surface, the battle is really between two national groups, the British and the Irish. The former happen to be Protestants and the latter Catholics, but the conflict is not primarily about religious matters, although the purely religious dimension has some importance too ... It is much more a struggle between two cultures unwilling to share the same territory.* 99

Fast track: The key questions

YOU WILL QUICKLY have realised from the previous page that this is a study of more than just the recent history of Northern Ireland. To see what caused 'the Troubles' to flare up in 1969 you will need to look at events much further back in history, well before the creation of Northern Ireland in 1922.

In the rest of this book you will be studying what we think are the key questions to investigate. Each chapter covers one theme, period or issue. Here is an outline view of what is included.

Q: Is the conflict really rooted in centuries-old historical problems?

In **Chapter 2** you will see that history has influenced Northern Ireland. You will see too that people have used history to suit their own purposes. However, you will also question the popular idea that conflict in Northern Ireland is inevitable because of its history.

Q: Why was Northern Ireland created in 1922?

In **Chapter 3** you will study how the rise of the nationalist movement in the late nineteenth century helped lead to the partition of Ireland in 1922 and the creation of Northern Ireland. You will consider why this happened even though neither side really wanted it.

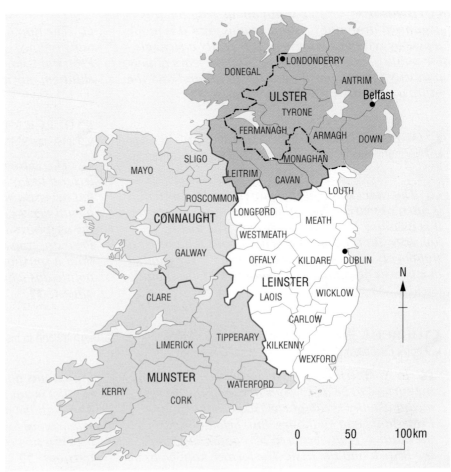

Q: Did Partition bring peace to Northern Ireland?

In **Chapter 4** you will investigate how Northern Ireland developed after Partition. You will see that it was relatively peaceful in the years 1922–67, but that there were many underlying problems which were being stored up for the future.

Q: Why did conflict break out in Northern Ireland in 1968–71?

In **Chapter 5** you will investigate how a small Nationalist-led 'CIVIL RIGHTS' march in 1968 escalated into violence, which triggered riots all over Northern Ireland. This in turn led to British troops being called in to keep the peace between nationalist and unionist communities.

Q: Why did attempts at peace fail in the 1970s and 1980s?

In **Chapter 6** you will see how 'tit-for-tat' paramilitary violence deepened the conflict and made Northern Ireland daily headline news around the world. You will examine how over two decades the British and Irish governments attempted but failed to achieve a political agreement between the warring parties. You will also see how Northern Ireland's politicians found it hard to compromise in order to achieve peace.

THE **AGREEMENT**

THIS AGREEMENT IS ABOUT <u>YOUR</u> FUTURE. PLEASE READ IT CAREFULLY.

It's Your Decision

Q: Is the conflict now over?

In **Chapter 7** you will examine the 1998 Good Friday Agreement and the factors which made it possible, while in **Chapter 8** you will look at the obstacles still in the way of peace and use your own up-to-the-minute research to decide how far the struggle for peace in Northern Ireland is now won.

■ ACTIVITY

Northern Ireland in the news

Northern Ireland can sometimes be a tricky subject to investigate, because the situation there changes regularly and in mainland Britain the coverage of news from Northern Ireland is very selective. Work in small groups to do a small-scale survey of how Northern Ireland is covered in the news on radio and TV, and in newspapers and other mass media.

Getting organised

1. Decide on the timescale for the news coverage you will look at (a week, two weeks, a month).
2. Decide what aspects of the Northern Ireland situation each member of your group will look at. This could include looking for references in news reports to

- the importance of past events (from the early twentieth century or before)
- the paramilitaries (could be divided into republican and loyalist paramilitaries)
- the involvement of other countries (particularly the USA)
- past attempts to secure peace (e.g. the Sunningdale Agreement)
- ordinary life.

3. Your group might decide to cover just one issue, and allocate different news sources between the members of the group to see how it is covered by different media.

   Whatever you choose you do need to work out your enquiry before you start. For example:
   a) what current events get most/least coverage in the media?
   b) how does the style and depth of coverage vary from medium to medium?
   c) what past event gets referred to most often in the media?
   d) does the media show a bias to one side or another?

Sources

Obvious sources include the radio and television news, and the daily newspapers.

The internet is also an excellent resource for studying Northern Ireland. Most of the main newspapers have their own internet sites. News organisations such as the BBC also have sites that provide news coverage, which can be searched for references to particular issues.

Recording and interpreting your findings

4. You could use an ICT database to record what you find out. Here is a possible structure.

Record Number:

Headline:

Date:

Publication or service:

Media type: (choose from Newspaper; Online; Radio; TV; Other)

Main article theme: (choose from Paramilitaries; Politics; Normal life; Security forces; British government; Irish government; USA; Other countries)

Brief summary of article:

Does the article make reference to history?: (choose from No reference; Recent (1970–90); Before 1970 (1922–69); Before Partition (any date before 1922)

Does the article have a bias in your opinion?: (choose from Unionist; Loyalist; Nationalist; Republican; Neutral)

---

5. When you have collated your data, you can search for patterns in the database to investigate, such as:
   a) Do different newspapers or other media focus on different issues?
   b) Do different media cover the same issues in different ways?
   c) Do particular events get the same amount of coverage?
   d) Do certain resources refer more or less frequently to past events?

You will also be able to think of many more questions to investigate once you have your database.

2 DOES IRISH HISTORY MAKE CONFLICT INEVITABLE?

> 66 To the Irish all history is applied history and the past is simply a convenient quarry which provides ammunition to use against enemies in the present. 99

> 66 It seems we must go back three centuries to explain any fight outside a chip shop. 99

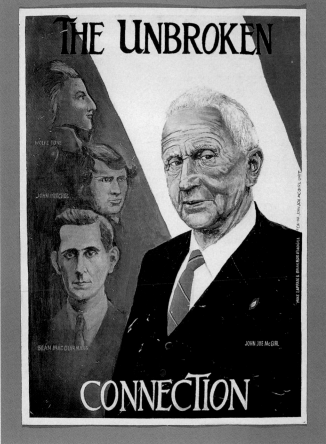

Selective history: 'Plantations, rebellions and massacres'

HISTORY IS STILL very powerful today in both Northern Ireland and the Republic.

- People involved in the conflict, including political parties, community organisations and paramilitary groups, often use history to support and justify their beliefs or their actions (or both).
- Observers of the conflict also look back at events in history as the best explanation for Northern Ireland's current divisions and conflicts. They assume that because Ireland has a long history of conflict that conflict is in some way inevitable. This might sound like a good explanation. It is certainly a common one. This is because the way that people involved in the conflict use history can feed the view that the people of the present day are simply refighting the battles of the past.

However, you will not be surprised that many historians think this view is mistaken. The view we take in this book is that **the problem is not history itself, but the way people use history**. We believe that there is an important difference between what actually happened in history and the way that history is used and interpreted, in particular the 'myths' that develop from it.

In this chapter you are going to look at some of the favourite heroes, villains and events in Irish history and see how groups or individuals use them. Although they might seem to have direct connections to the present conflict, if you look below the surface you see many contradictions which suggest that all is not as it seems. Nationalists or Unionists of the present day might suggest that they are still fighting the same battle as their predecessors, but in reality they often

- interpret history to suit their own views and ideas
- select bits of history which support their views and ignore events which do not fit.

Our view is that the story of the current conflict actually starts in the late nineteenth century, to which we come in Chapter 3, and that everything before that is important more because of the way it has been used than as a direct cause of the modern conflict.

SOURCE 1 A mural from a loyalist area of Belfast linking Cuchulainn with the loyalist paramilitary organisation the Ulster Defence Association (UDA). To the left there is a Bible. The shield has the red hand of Ulster on it. To the right is the badge of the UDA. Cuchulainn is sheltering the paramilitary

Two views of Cuchulainn

Cuchulainn (pronounced Coohullin) was a mythical CELTIC hero. The Celts were one of many waves of invaders and settlers who came to Ireland from prehistoric times onwards. One ancient Irish legend (the *Tain Bo Cualigne*) tells of a cattle raid on Ulster by raiders from other provinces of Ireland. In the story, the mighty Ulster hero Cuchulainn holds back the invading armies almost single-handedly. You might expect Cuchulainn to be an Ulster hero today, but, as Sources 1 and 2 show, it is not that simple.

■ TASK

1. Sources 1 and 2 are full of symbols. Explain each symbol. You can get a sheet from your teacher to help you.
2. Explain how the messages of Sources 1 and 2 are
a) different from each other
b) similar to each other.
3. Would you agree that the people who drew both murals are interpreting the story of Cuchulainn to suit their own ideas? Explain your answer.

SOURCE 2 A mural from a nationalist area of Belfast linking Cuchulainn with the present-day IRA and the EASTER RISING of 1916 (see pages 44–45). In the centre is a dedicated Celtic cross with the caption 'A tribute to the heroes of 1916'. The 1916 rising was a rebellion in Dublin by Republicans who wanted Ireland to be independent from the British Empire. Cuchulainn is shown on the right

Ireland in the sixteenth and seventeenth centuries

It is easy to see why some people believe the conflict goes back many centuries.

From the late 700s onwards, the various Irish peoples fought against Viking invaders.

From the late twelfth century, there was a similar process as Irish chieftains fought against Norman adventurers looking to carve out estates for themselves in Ireland.

From the Middle Ages, Ireland was in theory governed by the English monarch, although in practice the English monarch's authority was limited.

In the sixteenth and seventeenth centuries, there were major conflicts between Irish lords and English monarchs trying to gain more control of Ireland. In this period many influential events took place. Indeed, this is the period to which 'popular history' traces back the current conflict.

The sixteenth century: the Reformation

Throughout Europe in the early sixteenth century, arguments broke out between the Catholic Church and its critics (known as Protestants), who said that the Church was corrupt and out of touch with the lives of ordinary people. Protestants were put to death in Catholic countries, while in other states, whose governments had accepted Protestant teachings, Catholics suffered the same fate.

In England, King Henry VIII broke away from the Pope's control and declared himself head of the Church in England. Under Henry's son, Edward VI, England became a strongly Protestant state. Ireland, however, remained strongly Catholic. The majority of Irish people still saw the Pope in Rome as head of the 'true' Church. Conflict, sometimes full-scale war, between Catholics and Protestants was common around Europe for the next two centuries at least. The English were worried that Ireland would be used as a base by Catholics from Europe who might try to invade England. This resulted in conflict between English monarchs and Irish leaders throughout much of the century.

The seventeenth century: massacres and plantations

By 1602, the English Queen Elizabeth I had finally brought Ireland under English control. She was succeeded by James I in 1603, and in order to control Ireland he began the 'Plantation' of Ulster. This involved settling ('planting') Protestants from England and Scotland, loyal to the English Crown, on lands which had belonged to Irish Catholic opponents of the Crown.

Rebellion against English rule broke out in Ulster in 1641, and quickly spread to other parts of Ireland. Many Protestants were killed in brutal massacres. The highest death toll, in Ulster, included the alleged drowning of many Protestant settlers in Portadown (see Source 6, page 18). The rebels controlled Ireland for several years (1642–49), while the English were distracted by the English Civil War.

The English Protestant leader Oliver Cromwell restored English control of Ireland in 1649–50. His troops massacred both soldiers and civilians in Drogheda and Wexford. Catholics involved in the rebellion had their land confiscated, and were forced to emigrate or to live in the poor lands of Connacht. Many died of hunger and disease.

■ TASK

1. Here are four factors which have caused conflict in Ireland:

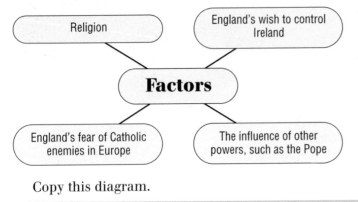

Copy this diagram.

2. Add to the diagram any examples in the text of occasions when the factors caused conflict.

3. Decide which has been the most serious cause of conflict. List the factors in order of importance in causing conflict.

4. It is easy to see the links between the current conflict and the events of the sixteenth and seventeenth centuries. Use Sources 3–5 to write a paragraph arguing that the roots of the present-day conflict in Northern Ireland lie in the sixteenth and seventeenth centuries. Think about how you would use each source to support your view. Save your answer. At the end of this chapter you will come to it and think about it again.

SOURCE 3 A Catholic propaganda print from 1587 showing the alleged treatment of Catholic priests by English forces in Ireland

SOURCE 4 The Plantation town of Magherafelt in Ulster in the early seventeenth century. Walled towns like this were built as strongholds from which the English and Scottish settlers (or Planters) could secure their hold on Ireland

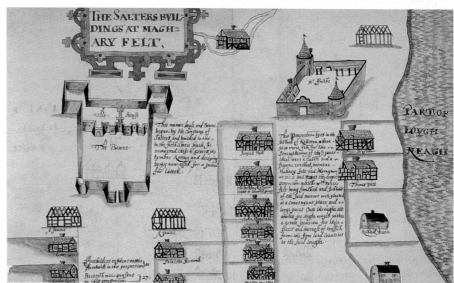

SOURCE 5 Part of the Down Survey of Ireland, 1654–55. The survey was carried out on the orders of Oliver Cromwell after his defeat of the Irish in 1649–50. The aim of the survey was to create an accurate picture of land ownership. This would help to dispossess Catholic rebels and give land to loyal Protestants

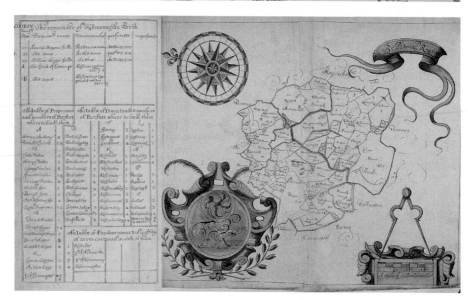

Two ways of looking at massacres

Plenty of the events described on the previous pages still have a big influence in Ireland.

If you went to Portadown in County Armagh, Northern Ireland, and said 'I am researching the massacres in the seventeenth century', people in the town would think they knew what you were talking about. The same would be true in Wexford, in the south-east corner of the Irish Republic.

However, the people of Portadown would probably assume you were researching the **massacre of Protestant settlers by Irish Catholics** who rebelled against English rule in 1641. The people of Wexford would probably assume you were talking about **the massacre of the Catholic troops and civilians of Wexford by Oliver Cromwell's Protestant troops** in 1649. They would be thinking of different massacres! However, sorting out this confusion is only the beginning of the historian's task. If the historian is to understand the links

between powerful events in the past such as these two massacres he or she must do two things:

a) understand the 'street history' view of events. Street history is the view of the ordinary person on the street, or in the home. It often appears in songs, on banners or on murals. Street history is not wrong, but often it is not the whole story

b) achieve his or her own more balanced view of this event, seeing it in its wider context alongside other events.

The real challenge lies in understanding, then looking beyond, the partial 'street history' version of events to the balanced historical view which puts the two massacres alongside each other to get a broader picture. Getting the whole story is important because the incomplete stories still have an impact on relations between the communities in Northern Ireland today.

Let's see how this might work.

THE MASSACRE OF PROTESTANTS BY IRISH CATHOLICS, 1641

The historian's view
The historian looking at the events of 1641 would try to present the complete picture:

- Catholics in Ulster resented losing their lands to the Protestant settlers. That resentment led to the rebellion and the massacres. This helps to explain the killings, but it does not justify them.
- The massacres were terrible: it is likely that between 2000 and 3000 Protestant settlers were killed. However, propaganda at the time exaggerated the massacres. One account of the time put the death toll at 154,000, even though there were probably not that many Protestants in Ulster at that time.

SOURCE 6 Irish rebels shown murdering Protestant captives in 1641. The picture comes from a book about the Irish rebellion. It was written by an English Protestant and published soon after the rebellion. It contained many gruesome images of what the rebels were supposed to have done. Many people believe the bridge shown in the picture is the same bridge that is standing in the centre of Portadown today, although some historians think that the seventeenth-century bridge was wooden

'Street history'
Protestant street history ignores the reasons for the rebellion. It also ignores the massacres of Catholics by Protestants in 1649. In some Protestant communities, the 1641 massacres are still used as evidence to support the view that all Catholics are bloodthirsty rebels who cannot be trusted.

Driuinge Men women & children by hund: reds vpon Briges & casting them into Riuers, who drowned not were killd with poles & shot with muskets.

■ TASK A

1. Look carefully at Source 6. Explain why someone in the 1640s
a) might want to draw and publish this image
b) might like to buy it and see it.
2. Explain how someone today could use this to support their view that Catholics cannot be trusted.

3. Explain why most historians would be very cautious about accepting Source 6 as a complete and accurate account of the events of 1641 in Portadown.

THE MASSACRE OF CATHOLICS BY OLIVER CROMWELL'S TROOPS, 1649

The historian's view
The historian looking at the events of 1649 faces similar problems.

- Historians try to stress that events such as the massacre in Wexford were not uncommon in Europe at that time. They were an accepted element of seventeenth-century warfare. They also happened in England during the Civil War.
- Historians also point out that Cromwell and his soldiers read and believed the propaganda about the massacres of Protestants. This helps to explain Cromwell's actions, but it does not justify them.

'Street history'
Nationalist street history ignores the historical context. It concentrates on the suffering Cromwell inflicted. Cromwell is still a figure of hate in parts of Ireland today. Source 7 expresses this view. The 1649 massacres have made it easy to motivate many young people to join republican movements, including those which support violence (see Source 4 on page 29).

SOURCE 7 The chorus of a song written in 1989 by the Pogues. There are many Irish folk songs about Cromwell, and virtually all of them express similar views to this one

66 *A curse upon you Oliver Cromwell*
You who raped our Motherland
I hope you're rotting down in Hell
For the horrors that you sent
To our misfortunate forefathers
Whom you robbed of their birthright
'To Hell or Connacht' may you burn in Hell tonight. 99

■ TASK B

1. Look at Source 7. Explain why
a) a songwriter in the 1980s might want to write this
b) a listener might like to listen to or buy this song.
2. Explain how someone today could use this to support their view that Protestants cannot be trusted.
3. Does Source 7 present the same problems for the historian as Source 6? Explain your answer.

The big idea
History is complicated. A balanced view is hard to achieve. It is also sometimes less interesting than the biased view! Many people don't want to have a balanced view. They prefer to use history to support their own viewpoint.

On pages 20–27 you are going to look at a further two major case-studies of re-interpreted or selective use of history.

Case study 1: Who was the real William of Orange?

EVERY SUMMER, THOUSANDS of Protestants take part in marches and carry banners with images of William of Orange (King William III of England) on them. Most of the marches are organised by the Loyal Orange Order, which is named after him. As a result, the majority of Protestants in Northern Ireland would not find it too hard to tell you a few important things about William of Orange:

- William is a hero to Protestants in Ireland. He rescued them from being driven out by their Catholic enemies.
- William's victory over the Catholics at the Battle of the Boyne in 1690 made Protestant control of Ireland secure.
- Protestants and Unionists have always celebrated William's victories as safeguarding Irish Protestantism and political freedom.

William of Orange, Derry and the Boyne

The trouble with this view is that, while it is not wrong, it is not quite the whole story. The drawing below shows some of the events that do not quite fit this picture of William of Orange. The full story certainly involves William and Ireland, but it also involves England, Holland and France. It even includes the head of the Roman Catholic Church, the Pope.

SOURCE 1 A mural from a unionist area of Belfast

SOURCE 2 A celebration mug marking the 200th anniversary of the Orange Order which commemorates William of Orange

Some of the events of 1690

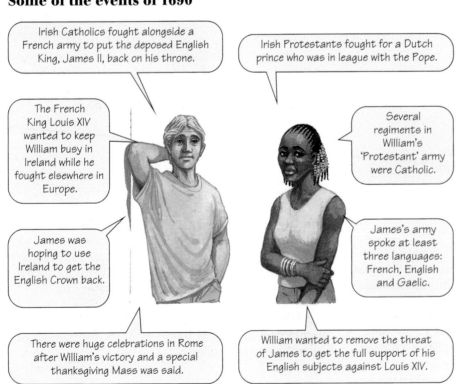

Irish Catholics fought alongside a French army to put the deposed English King, James II, back on his throne.

The French King Louis XIV wanted to keep William busy in Ireland while he fought elsewhere in Europe.

James was hoping to use Ireland to get the English Crown back.

There were huge celebrations in Rome after William's victory and a special thanksgiving Mass was said.

Irish Protestants fought for a Dutch prince who was in league with the Pope.

Several regiments in William's 'Protestant' army were Catholic.

James's army spoke at least three languages: French, English and Gaelic.

William wanted to remove the threat of James to get the full support of his English subjects against Louis XIV.

■ ACTIVITY

Work in pairs. Imagine you have to prepare a short essay on 'Who was the real William of Orange?'

You have three points to start you off:

- William was a Protestant.
- William defeated Ireland's Catholics at the Battle of the Boyne.
- Protestants in Ireland have always honoured William of Orange.

With your partner, search for three more points which could be added to provide a more complete picture. Use the information here and on pages 21–23.

Your teacher may ask you to compare your work in this Activity with your work from the Activity on page 24 (Wolfe Tone).

The story of King Billy: Part one 1688–89

The full story begins in England in 1688. The Catholic King of England, James II, was causing great concern to his mainly Protestant subjects. Most Protestants felt that the Catholic Church threatened both political and religious liberty. People in the seventeenth century did not separate these two ideas. They believed the Church would not tolerate any religious ideas other than its own. They also felt that in Catholic countries the Church had too much political power and influence.

1 James tended to ignore his Parliament and make decisions on his own.

2 Leading Protestant nobles in England rebelled against James and deposed him. They did this to protect their liberty (as they saw it).

3 The nobles asked James's Protestant daughter Mary and her husband William of Orange (in the Netherlands) to rule instead of James.

4 Meanwhile, James fled to France. Louis XIV was a close friend of James, and the bitter enemy of William of Orange. Louis supplied James with troops and ships to help get his throne back.

5 Instead of invading England, James landed in Ireland in March 1689. He thought he could get the support of Catholics in Ireland to increase his strength.

6 At first, things went well for James and his supporters (JACOBITES). Soon only north-west Ulster held out, desperately awaiting aid from William.

7 The key was the city of Londonderry. As James approached the city, it almost fell without a fight. The commander of the city guard thought the situation was hopeless.

8 Then at the last moment thirteen apprentice boys shut the gates of the city as the Jacobites approached.

9 A long siege followed from April to July 1689. Londonderry's citizens suffered terribly, but they held out and in doing so became part of Protestant legend.

The story of King Billy: Part two 1689–95

SOURCE 3 A loyalist mural from the Fountain area of Londonderry, showing the relief of the siege

10 The siege of Londonderry bought enough time for William to bring his forces to Ireland. These included troops sent by the head of the Roman Catholic Church, Pope Alexander.

11 William defeated James at the Battle of the Boyne in July 1690. However, the Jacobite forces were not finally defeated until the following year.

Treaty

1. 15,000 of James' soldiers can go safely to France.
2. Catholics in Ireland can keep their lands if they promise to be loyal to William.
3. No extra limits on Catholics' freedom to worship.

12 The war officially ended with the Treaty of Limerick of October 1691. It was extremely generous for the times.

> William must take measures to make our power more secure.

13 However, Protestants in Ireland were unhappy about the Treaty. They forced William to take measures which would make Protestant power in Ireland even more secure.

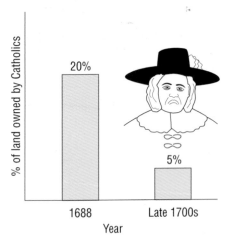

14 In the seventeenth century power meant owning the land. Over the next 100 years Catholic land holdings fell from about twenty per cent of the land in 1688 to about five per cent in the late eighteenth century.

own property   be educated

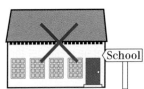

own weapons   work as a lawyer or in government

15 Catholics also suffered from the Penal Laws passed in 1695. These restricted Catholic rights to own property, to be educated, to own weapons or to work in the law or government.

■ TASK

1. Explain why William was keen to take the English throne.
2. Explain why James landed in Ireland.
3. 'The siege of Londonderry is remembered today because it is such a dramatic story.' Do you agree, or is there more to it than this?
4. What do the terms of the Treaty of Limerick suggest about William's attitude to Catholics?
5. 'William's campaigns in Ireland were part of both an Irish conflict and a European conflict.' Do you agree with this statement? Explain your answer by referring to events mentioned in the story strip on pages 21–22.

The story of King Billy: Part three, 1695–present

King Billy's victory at the Boyne is celebrated in marches and on murals today, 300 years after the events that made him famous.

Most people think that Protestants have always remembered William of Orange and the Battle of the Boyne with parades and marches. However, the full picture is not as simple as that. When we look at how William and the events connected with him have been commemorated, we find some unexpected facts.

- From the end of the seventeenth century until 1806, William's birthday was an official holiday. Despite this, there is very little evidence of any parades or celebrations on this date in the 1700s, even in 1790, the 100th anniversary of the Battle of the Boyne.
- The Battle of the Boyne was celebrated in Downpatrick and Doagh in 1790, but as a triumph of liberty over bad (British) government, not a religious victory. A toast was drunk to the American Revolution – a British defeat!
- On the centenary of the siege of Londonderry in 1790, the parade included lots of Catholics. The Catholic bishop went to the service in the Protestant Church of Ireland cathedral.
- The Apprentice Boys of Londonderry, who organise marches to commemorate the part played by apprentices in the siege of Londonderry, were not founded until the early 1800s.
- The Orange Order was founded in memory of William of Orange more than 100 years after the Battle of the Boyne, after a gun battle in County Armagh in 1795 between the Defenders (a Catholic underground resistance movement) and the Peep o' Days Boys (a Protestant organisation).
- In 1790, the Northern Whigs, a group of well-off Protestants who wanted England to have less control over Irish affairs, celebrated William's birthday.

What does all this mean in terms of the conflict in Northern Ireland today? Well, it seems to suggest that some groups or people have been selective in their use of history. The King Billy story, far from laying the foundations for the current conflict, was brought back to life by groups to give some historical backing to their struggle – but they only took the bits of the story which suited them.

- In the early 1700s, William was remembered with respect, but Protestants did not feel threatened by Catholics. That is why William's victory was not really celebrated for most of the eighteenth century.
- In the late eighteenth century, tensions were rising in Ulster and the rest of Ireland. In Armagh violent fights between Catholic and Protestant gangs were common. The Orange Order 'revived' their own version of William of Orange as a Protestant hero. However, **they ignored** the awkward facts such as the large number of Catholic troops in William's army at the Boyne and that William had the full support of the Pope.
- In the 1790s, some Republicans (Catholics and PRESBYTERIAN Protestants) in Ulster wanted to cut the links between England and Ireland. They 'revived' the William of Orange who believed in the idea of liberty. However, **they ignored** the awkward fact that William was King of England and had helped to strengthen the tie between England and Ireland in the first place.
- In the 1880s, Ulster Protestants feared that the HOME RULE movement (see pages 36–40) would achieve its aims and that they would be ruled by a hostile parliament in Dublin. They 'revived' King William as a defender of Protestantism and liberty. However, **they ignored** awkward facts such as the Treaty of Limerick, in which William upset his Protestant Irish subjects when he offered generous terms to his defeated Catholic enemies. (William thought it was a better way to keep Ireland stable and secure.) They also **ignored** the fact that William was not much interested in Ireland. For him the Battle of the Boyne was only one part of a European conflict between himself and his bitter rival Louis XIV of France.

By this stage, you might feel pretty irritated with William of Orange, or even me, for making the story so complicated! However, think again. Am I the problem, or is it the people who have chosen the bits of William's story which suit them and ignored the rest?

Case study 2: Why is Wolfe Tone a republican hero?

A QUICK LOOK AT Sources 1–4 would seem to answer the question of why Wolfe Tone is a republican hero. Most Republicans regard Tone as the first Irish Republican. Some also admire the fact that he was prepared to use force to separate England from Ireland. Many Republicans would be able to tell you the following facts about Wolfe Tone:

■ He was a committed campaigner for equal rights for Catholics in Ireland.
■ He was a leading figure in the United Irishmen movement of the 1790s.
■ He was exiled from Ireland for his beliefs.
■ He gained French help for the Irish rebellion in 1798, which seriously threatened British rule for a time.

However, it will not surprise you that there are complications to this story, too. Let's look in more detail at the Wolfe Tone story.

■ ACTIVITY

Work in pairs. Imagine you have to prepare a short essay with the title 'Who was the real Theobald Wolfe Tone?'

You have three points to start you off:

■ Wolfe Tone campaigned for the rights of Catholics.
■ He was prepared to use force to break the link between England and Ireland.
■ Nationalists and Republicans in Ireland have always honoured Wolfe Tone.

With your partner, search for three more points which could be added to provide a more complete picture. Refer to the information and sources here and on pages 25–27.

Your teacher may ask you to compare your work in this Activity with your work from the Activity on page 20 (William of Orange).

SOURCE 1 'The Unbroken Connection', an Irish–American republican fundraising poster from the early 1990s. The figures linked with Wolfe Tone were all republican activists in the nineteenth and twentieth centuries

SOURCE 2 An advertisement from the front page of the republican newspaper *An Phoblacht*, June 1982

SOURCE 3 A republican mug commemorating Wolfe Tone and the 1798 rebellion

SOURCE 4 Wolfe Tone

66 My aims were to break the connection with England and to assert the independence of my country.

My methods were to unite the whole people of Ireland, to abolish the memory of all past disputes, and to replace names like Protestant, Catholic and Dissenter with the name of Irishman. 99

Wolfe Tone and the United Irishmen

Theobald Wolfe Tone was a Protestant Dublin lawyer – not the most obvious background for a republican hero. At first, he was not much of a rebel, either. He was part of what became known as the Protestant Ascendancy. This was the name given to the period in the eighteenth and nineteenth centuries when Protestants were supreme in Ireland. They dominated the parliament in Dublin. They owned most of the land, made the laws and held the best jobs in government. You could hardly expect Tone, as part of this powerful elite, to be a rebel. However, in the 1790s Tone found himself the leader of an unlikely alliance called the UNITED IRISHMEN. This was formed from three different groups, each of which had reason to be unhappy about the way Ireland was ruled.

Anglican Protestants

Many middle-class ANGLICAN Protestants (like Tone) found that they could not make progress in their careers. This was because their families did not have English connections or influence in high places.

Catholics

Catholics resented the restrictions placed on them by the Penal Laws (see Source 5).

> ## SOURCE 5 The Penal Laws against Catholics, 1695
>
> - *Catholics could not bear arms.*
> - *Catholic children could not be educated.*
> - *Catholics could not own a horse valued at above £5.*
> - *Catholic archbishops and bishops had to leave Ireland.*
> - *Priests were not replaced when they died.*
> - *Catholics could not buy property.*
> - *On the death of the owner, Catholic estates had to be divided equally between sons (although if a son became a Protestant he got all the land).*
> - *Catholics could not have leases on land over 32 years.*
> - *No Catholics could be lawyers, army officers or public officials.*
> - *Catholics could not vote or be MPs.*

Tone felt that measures such as the Penal Laws kept Irish people divided, and that England wanted this. In August 1791 he published a political pamphlet called *An Argument on Behalf of the Catholics of Ireland.* He argued that Catholics should be free from all restrictions and should be treated in the same way as Protestants. The pamphlet made Tone famous throughout Ireland, launched his career as a political writer and made him a popular figure with Catholics.

Presbyterians

Presbyterian Protestants also suffered a range of restrictions under the Penal Laws (see Source 6).

> ## SOURCE 6 Penal Laws against Presbyterians (also called Dissenters) passed in 1695
>
> - *Presbyterians had to pay taxes to the Anglican Church.*
> - *Presbyterian marriages could be ruled illegal – this meant children could be declared illegitimate.*
> - *Presbyterians could not be civil servants, town councillors or army officers.*
> - *Presbyterians could not vote or become MPs.*

Most Presbyterians lived in Ulster. Discontent was strongest in Belfast, where in the 1780s several political groups began campaigning for changes in the laws and system of government. They invited Wolfe Tone to come and speak to them. In August 1791, they formed a movement called the United Irishmen.

The United Irishmen

Membership of this movement spread across Ireland. In Ulster it was made up of Presbyterians and Catholics, while in the rest of Ireland the members were mostly Catholics.

At this point it is important to be clear about what the United Irishmen wanted. The movement was meant to bring all the discontented groups together to campaign for reforms. Its main demands were:

- ending the Penal Laws against Catholics and Presbyterians
- reforming the Irish parliament in Dublin so that it would represent the people of Ireland fairly, and so that jobs in government would be gained on ability rather than through family connections
- ending the right of parliament in London to block laws passed by the Dublin parliament.

The United Irishmen saw themselves as defenders of liberty against bad government. They were reformers. They were definitely not republicans or revolutionaries. However, they were inspired by the revolutions which had taken place in America (1776–83) and in France (1789). They felt that these revolutions had overthrown bad governments and given freedom to people like them.

Wolfe Tone and the 1798 rebellion

To start with, the campaign of the United Irishmen had some important successes. For example, in 1792 Catholics were allowed to be lawyers, and in 1793 they gained the right to vote.

However, the attitude of the government in London soon changed. From 1792 onwards, Britain was at war with revolutionary France. The government was frightened of revolution spreading to Britain. Radical reformers like Tone were now seen as potential traitors, and the government clamped down on them brutally.

When Tone was caught negotiating with a French spy, he was forced to leave the country. This was a severe blow for the United Irishmen. It also turned Tone from a reformer into a revolutionary.

He went to America, but soon moved to France, where his aim was to gain French support for an Irish rebellion. He succeeded. In December 1796 he was part of a French invasion fleet which tried to land in Ireland but was defeated by bad weather.

The 1798 rebellion

In Ulster, the clampdown on the United Irishmen continued. Discontent simmered. Then, in the summer of 1798, when the British turned their attention to the rest of Ireland, the country exploded into rebellion.

The largest-scale fighting was in County Wexford and in Ulster. In Ulster, the mainly Presbyterian United Irish forces fought against British soldiers. The rebels outnumbered the government forces, but they were disorganised and poorly equipped. Source 7 shows the level of support for the rebellion in Ulster, and why it caused such concern for the British government.

Wolfe Tone spent many frustrating months trying to get the French to aid the rebels. Finally, a force set sail in August 1798 and landed in County Mayo. Another force, including Wolfe Tone himself, sailed in September. However, it was too little too late. The rebellion had already largely collapsed by mid-June. Tone was captured and sentenced to death. He killed himself in jail on 19 November 1798.

Cruelty

Both sides behaved with great cruelty towards their opponents. In Ulster, more Protestants were killed by the British forces in 1798 than were killed by Catholics in the rebellion and massacres of 1641 (see pages 18–19). In Wexford, Protestant prisoners were massacred by the rebels. In turn, these massacres were followed by brutal reprisals by the British forces against the rebels. Many innocent Catholics were killed in the process.

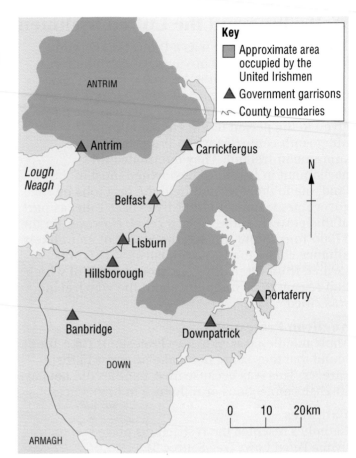

SOURCE 7 The extent of rebel control of Ulster during the 1798 rebellion

A turning point?

After the rebellion, the attitude of Ulster Presbyterian Protestants began to change. A combination of defeat in battle, the repression which followed the rebellion and the news of massacres of Protestants by Catholics in the rest of Ireland convinced most Ulster Protestants that their future now lay in loyalty to a Protestant United Kingdom.

The events of 1798 played an important role in forming the current loyalist attitudes of Ulster Presbyterians.

■ TASK

Many people who know little about Irish history might be surprised to learn that Ulster Protestants played a leading role in the rebellion against the British government. Explain

a) why it was that these Protestants played a leading role in the rebellion

b) why people might find this information surprising.

How have Nationalists and Republicans remembered Wolfe Tone?

Tone began his career as a lawyer. Frustration made him a political writer. This led to him becoming a reformer. It took the actions of a government to turn him into a rebel. However, that is not quite how Nationalists have remembered him.

Tone was buried at Bodenstown, County Kildare. Local Nationalists treated the grave as a kind of shrine, but it was some time before Nationalists all over Ireland began to see Tone as a hero. The Young Ireland nationalist movement first published his life and his deeds in the 1840s, but it was not until the 1890s that Tone was well established as a nationalist hero. However, as Source 8 explains, he meant different things to different people.

SOURCE 8 From *Wolfe Tone, Prophet of Irish Independence*, by Marianne Elliott, a leading expert on Tone

❝ *Tone's reputation as the 'father' of Irish republicanism is accepted by every political grouping in Ireland. But each takes from the Tone tradition only what it needs to sustain its own stance.*

The celebrations of 1898 ... gave rise to Sinn Fein, the republican Dungannon Clubs and most of all the revival of the IRISH REPUBLICAN BROTHERHOOD [IRB] ... Within a few years the Wolfe Tone Memorial Committee had become a front for the IRB and Bodenstown the symbol of militant republicanism. ❞

In 1898, Irish Nationalists commemorated the centenary of the rebellion. Those who believed in peaceful struggle emphasised Tone's desire to unite all the people of Ireland. More militant, republican Nationalists highlighted Tone's willingness to use physical force and his wish to separate Ireland from England completely. Eventually, Tone's struggle and death became an inspiration for militant Republicans.

So we see that Wolfe Tone has gone through a similar process to William of Orange. The real Wolfe Tone, with all the awkward complications, was not a good enough symbol for Republicans after his death.

- Until the 1840s, there were very few commemorations or ceremonies involving Wolfe Tone.
- The Young Ireland movement 'revived' Wolfe Tone in the 1840s. Young Ireland was a radical nationalist movement which was prepared to use force to make Ireland independent from Britain.

SOURCE 9 The print on a handkerchief produced in 1898 to commemorate the centenary of the 1798 rebellion. Lord Edward Fitzgerald was a leading member of the United Irishmen. Henry Joy McCracken was one of the United Irishmen's leaders in Ulster. Daniel O'Connell and Robert Emmett were nationalist leaders in the early nineteenth century. O'Connell was totally opposed to violence and would not have been pleased to see himself linked to Tone and Fitzgerald

- In the late nineteenth and early twentieth centuries, a new generation of hardline Republicans like Eamon de Valera emerged (see page 43). They were determined to use armed force to end British rule in Ireland, and believed that Ireland should be Catholic and Irish. They saw Wolfe Tone as their inspiration.
- Wolfe Tone is a hero for the present-day republican party Sinn Fein, whose members visit his grave each year (see Source 2, page 24).

All these movements have ignored several awkward facts about Wolfe Tone:

- One of his key aims was to create unity and understanding between Protestants and Catholics in Ireland.
- He was a very reluctant revolutionary and only saw armed rebellion as a last resort.
- He was a Protestant.

So, Wolfe Tone did not set the current conflict off on its current lines any more than King Billy did (see page 23). Wolfe Tone did not lay its foundations. Rather, just like King Billy, the story of Wolfe Tone is the historical quarry people mine (selectively) when they need historical backing for their current struggle.

Is history really the problem in Northern Ireland?

If William of Orange gave Protestants liberty, why did he introduce Penal Laws to restrict their freedom?

So let's get this straight. Wolfe Tone, a Protestant, is a Catholic hero for his role in the rebellion of 1798 ... But he spent most of that year in France or on a boat.

If today's SECTARIAN conflict goes back to the seventeenth century, how come Presbyterians and Catholics fought together in 1798?

As we have seen, some people believe that the current sectarian conflict in Ireland goes back hundreds of years. You may have begun to doubt this.

Analysing the story of William of Orange probably left you feeling a bit confused as to who was on whose side. Wolfe Tone's story may have raised even more questions. You should by now have realised that Ireland's history is much more complex than the idea that Catholic Nationalists and Protestant Unionists have been slugging it out since the 1600s or even before.

There are plenty of examples of co-operation between Catholics and Protestants. Many Presbyterians joined Catholic priests in campaigns to improve conditions for Catholic Irish peasants in the period 1850–80. The *County Down Recorder* of 4 July 1868 covers the story of Ballynahinch Catholic church, built with the help of contributions from Protestants. Indeed, on the whole, people have spent most of their time just living normal lives, and not thinking about sectarian issues at all.

Of course, there are patterns for the current conflict in the past. For example, for eight centuries the question of whether Britain should control Ireland has divided and united communities. That was the question in the seventeenth and eighteenth centuries, and it is the question now. Until it is sorted out conclusively, conflict is always possible.

The past also contains some of the basic ingredients of the current conflict: sectarian groups, marginalised majorities, powerful minorities and divisive tendencies. However, and this is the key point, **the fact that such patterns exist does not make conflict inevitable**. Historians point out that many countries, including Belgium, the Netherlands, Germany, Italy and Norway, have had national or religious divisions (or both) which go back many hundreds of years. In these countries, people now manage to live peacefully.

The temptation on finding such patterns in Northern Ireland is to think they offer a tidy explanation for the present conflict. But this book maintains that sectarian tension or nationalist ambitions do not make a conflict inevitable. To explain the current conflict we need to look at events closer to the present day. These are what you will study in Chapters 3, 4 and 5.

However, we are still left with the problem of people's views of history. Irish history in the sixteenth to eighteenth centuries is a potent mix of violence, injustice and frustration, which could fuel a hundred arguments and often does. While you cannot say that the current conflict is caused by the past, you could say that one real problem is the way people use history to back up their point of view. Look at Sources 1–7 and see what you think.

SOURCE 1 Dermot Bolger, an Irish novelist

❝ *It seems we must go back three centuries to explain any fight outside a chip shop.* ❞

SOURCE 2 Dr A.T.Q. Stewart, a leading Irish historian

❝ *To the Irish all history is applied history and the past is simply a convenient quarry which provides ammunition to use against enemies in the present.* ❞

SOURCE 3 The *Irish News*, December 1991

❝ *Indeed many of the troubles which beset Ireland at this end of the twentieth century have been caused by those who believe it is more important to build a country fit for our ancestors rather than our children.*

It has become popular to blame history for our present situation. But the real blame lies with the tunnel vision of those who prefer to take a partial view of the history of this island. These people are in a tiny minority, yet by exploiting the fears of others they have gained the initiative. ❞

SOURCE 4 Shane O'Doherty, an IRA volunteer in the 1970s, explains why he joined the IRA

❝ *My attraction to the IRA was not initially based on the sight or experience of any particular social injustice ... It was the discovery of the tragedies of Irish history ... and the best part of that history I imbibed alone at home reading books in the family library. It was the pure political injustice of British rule in Ireland against the wishes of the Irish people which fired my anger ...* ❞

SOURCE 5 The Coroner of Sligo (in the Irish Republic), commenting on the inquest into the death of Earl Mountbatten, killed by an IRA bomb in 1979

❝ *I believe it is necessary to stress again the great responsibility that parents and teachers of any nation have in the way they interpret history and pass it on to the youth of their country. I believe that if history could be taught in such a fashion that it would help to create harmony among people rather than division and hatred, it would serve this nation and all other nations better.* ❞

SOURCE 6 An extract from the *Church of Ireland Gazette* of January 1995 explaining how loyalist paramilitaries use history to explain their actions

❝ *Loyalist paramilitarism sees itself as the guardian of an inherited sacred trust, linked in a direct line back to their forefathers who over and over again have barricaded themselves into their chosen territory and shouted defiance from where they stood with an ancestral gun in their hands.* ❞

SOURCE 7 An extract from *Dancing to History's Tune* by Brian Walker, Director of the Institute of Irish Studies of Queen's University, Belfast

❝ *If one believes that the struggle between the two major groups in Northern Ireland has been continuous since early times, then it is difficult to see a resolution to our problems. This sense of history is inadequate because it fails to take into account quiet times. When we appreciate the European perspective on the situation, we realise that these difficulties are not unique to us and unavoidable because of some special historical roots. This means that our current conflicts are not inevitable nor insoluble due to our remote past.* ❞

■ TASK A

'It's not history that's the problem, it's the way people use it.' How convincing do you find this view? Explain your answer in terms of

■ the way Unionists have used history
■ the way Nationalists have used history.

Write a paragraph for each one. You could do extra research if you wish.

■ TASK B

Look back at the paragraph you wrote on page 16. Now prepare a reply to the statement below.

The roots of the present-day conflict in Northern Ireland lie in the sixteenth and seventeenth centuries.

■ REVIEW TASK AND ASSIGNMENT

Some Irish historians have pointed out that today Irish history is not widely studied in Northern Ireland or the Republic. They are concerned about this, because it means most people know only popular history. This is picked up in the home or from songs or poems, or from the murals in loyalist or republican areas.

Work in small groups. Your task is to advise the government of Northern Ireland or the Republic on the following question:

Why is it important for students in
Northern Ireland and the Republic
to study history?

You must produce a report based on this question. Your report must explain:

■ how evidence has been used or interpreted selectively (give examples)
■ how this use of evidence can lead to problems and even conflict (give examples)
■ how teaching the whole, complicated story of the real context of these sources can help to reduce some of these problems.

Your report should include:

■ an example of nationalist or republican selective history
■ an example of unionist or loyalist selective history
■ at least one written source
■ at least one visual source (this may include murals).

Your teacher can advise you on other resources if you wish to take your research further.

POBLACHT NA H EIREANN.

THE PROVISIONAL GOVERNMENT
OF THE
IRISH REPUBLIC
TO THE PEOPLE OF IRELAND.

IRISHMEN AND IRISHWOMEN : In the name of God and of the dead generations from which she receives her old tradition of nationhood, Ireland, through us, summons her children to her flag and strikes for her freedom.

Having organised and trained her manhood through her secret revolutionary organisation, the Irish Republican Brotherhood, and through her open military organisations, the Irish Volunteers and the Irish Citizen Army, having patiently perfected her discipline, having resolutely waited for the right moment to reveal itself, she now seizes that moment, and, supported by her exiled children in America and by gallant allies in Europe, but relying in the first on her own strength, she strikes in full confidence of victory.

We declare the right of the people of Ireland to the ownership of Ireland, and to the unfettered control of Irish destinies, to be sovereign and indefeasible. The long usurpation of that right by a foreign people and government has not extinguished the right, nor can it ever be extinguished except by the destruction of the Irish people. In every generation the Irish people have asserted their right to national freedom and sovereignty; six times during the past three hundred years they have asserted it in arms. Standing on that fundamental right and again asserting it in arms in the face of the world, we hereby proclaim the Irish Republic as a Sovereign Independent State, and we pledge our lives and the lives of our comrades-in-arms to the cause of its freedom, of its welfare, and of its exaltation among the nations.

The Irish Republic is entitled to, and hereby claims, the allegiance of every Irishman and Irishwoman. The Republic guarantees religious and civil liberty, equal rights and equal opportunities to all its citizens, and declares its resolve to pursue the happiness and prosperity of the whole nation and of all its parts, cherishing all the children of the nation equally, and oblivious of the differences carefully fostered by an alien government, which have divided a minority from the majority in the past.

Until our arms have brought the opportune moment for the establishment of a permanent National Government, representative of the whole people of Ireland and elected by the suffrages of all her men and women, the Provisional Government, hereby constituted, will administer the civil and military affairs of the Republic in trust for the people.

We place the cause of the Irish Republic under the protection of the Most High God, Whose blessing we invoke upon our arms, and we pray that no one who serves that cause will dishonour it by cowardice, inhumanity, or rapine. In this supreme hour the Irish nation must, by its valour and discipline and by the readiness of its children to sacrifice themselves for the common good, prove itself worthy of the august destiny to which it is called.

Signed on Behalf of the Provisional Government,
THOMAS J. CLARKE,
SEAN Mac DIARMADA, THOMAS MacDONAGH,
P. H. PEARSE, EAMONN CEANNT,
JAMES CONNOLLY, JOSEPH PLUNKETT.

Ulster's
Solemn League and Covenant.

Being convinced in our consciences that Home Rule would be disastrous to the material well-being of Ulster as well as of the whole of Ireland, subversive of our civil and religious freedom, destructive of our citizenship and perilous to the unity of the Empire, we, whose names are under-written, men of Ulster, loyal subjects of His Gracious Majesty King George V., humbly relying on the God whom our fathers in days of stress and trial confidently trusted, do hereby pledge ourselves in solemn Covenant throughout this our time of threatened calamity to stand by one another in defending for ourselves and our children our cherished position of equal citizen-ship in the United Kingdom and in using all means which may be found necessary to defeat the present conspiracy to set up a Home Rule Parliament in Ireland. ¶ And in the event of such a Parliament being forced upon us we further solemnly and mutually pledge ourselves to refuse to recognise its authority. ¶ In sure confidence that God will defend the right we hereto subscribe our names. ¶ And further, we individually declare that we have not already signed this Covenant.

The above was signed by me at
"Ulster Day," Saturday, 28th September, 1912.

—— God Save the King. ——

Fast track: The Partition of Ireland, 1922

DURING THIS COURSE, you are trying to see the modern conflict in Northern Ireland in its historical context. In Chapter 2 we discussed how far back in history we need to go to see the origins of the conflict, and questioned the idea that the current conflict goes back to the sixteenth or seventeenth centuries. However, we now come to a period that is much more important. Many historians feel that the real roots of the present conflict are in the period 1880–1922. In this period

- the unionist and nationalist movements emerged
- both movements armed themselves, and signalled they were ready to use violence to achieve their aims
- following a bitter war, the British government partitioned Ireland in 1922 and created Northern Ireland.

An overview of these developments is given on pages 32–4.

Unionists v Nationalists: armed conflict

In 1801, the government in London passed the Act of Union. This meant that Ireland was ruled directly by Parliament in London. From that point until the early 1920s, the biggest political issue in Ireland was the argument between Unionists, who supported the Union between Britain and Ireland, and Nationalists, who wanted to end it.

Unionists wanted to keep Ireland as part of the United Kingdom. By 1914, it was clear they were prepared to use force to achieve this.

Some Unionists in Ulster would fight government troops, Irish Nationalists or anyone else who threatened their political and religious freedom. The most spectacular demonstration of this was the so-called Larne gun running. On 24–25 April 1914, the Ulster Volunteer Force landed a huge shipment of illegal arms at the port of Larne. It was hardly a secret. Almost every motor car in County Antrim at that time was involved in the operation. The arms were driven away and hidden.

SOURCE 1 An image from the *Illustrated London News* of the Larne gun running, when Unionists illegally imported arms at Larne, County Antrim, on 24–25 April 1914

■ ACTIVITY

You have seen several examples of how different groups in Ireland have used visual imagery to win support for their cause. Look carefully at Sources 1 and 4. Explain how the details of each source try to make statements such as:

- 'Our movement has the people behind it!'
- 'We are prepared to fight for our cause!'
- 'We will never surrender!'

Nationalists wanted all of Ireland to be independent of Britain. Like Unionists they were prepared to use force to achieve their aims.

During the Great War of 1914–18, most Nationalists stopped campaigning against British rule in Ireland. However, on Easter Monday 1916, extreme republican Nationalists took over parts of central Dublin. They declared that Ireland was an independent republic. The Rising lasted only a week, but the fighting killed or injured many civilians. It wrecked the centre of Dublin. Although it was quickly crushed, the Easter Rising became an inspirational event for Republicans and encouraged further violent resistance to British rule.

SOURCE 2 The shattered remains of the Dublin General Post Office. This was the headquarters of the rebels in 1916

SOURCE 3 A postcard commemorating the Easter Rising

SOURCE 4 A painting of the occupation of the GPO building in Dublin by leaders of the Easter Rising of 1916. This romanticised representation of events was created soon after the event by supporters of the IRB

The Partition of Ireland: Violent campaigns against British rule continued after 1916 and reached a peak in the years 1919–21. There was a bitter GUERRILLA war between the Irish Republican Army (IRA) and British forces. In late 1921, the Republicans and the British government agreed a truce. Although the British forces were not defeated, the attitude of the government to the conflict changed. By 1921 it felt that a single Ireland, ruled by Britain, was not worth fighting for. Partition seemed the best solution to the ongoing conflict.

Discussions between the Republicans and the British government resulted in the Anglo–Irish Treaty of 1921 and the Partition of Ireland in 1922. Source 5 shows the results of the treaty. (Page 49 goes into greater detail.)

Controversy

The treaty was deeply controversial. Here are just a few reasons why.

■ Most Unionists did not want Partition. They wanted the whole of Ireland to remain part of the United Kingdom.

■ Partition left many Unionists living in the newly created Irish Free State, although most of them wanted to remain part of the United Kingdom.

■ Partition left a substantial nationalist population living in the new state of Northern Ireland. Most of them wanted to be part of the Irish Free State.

■ Even Nationalists and Republicans in Ireland did not want Partition. They wanted all of Ireland (including the counties which were made into Northern Ireland) to be independent of Britain. The Irish leaders Michael Collins and Arthur Griffith, who had agreed to Partition, soon faced a civil war against other Nationalists who thought that Partition was an unacceptable compromise. Collins was killed in that war.

Why did it happen?

So the big question for the historian is: if neither Nationalists nor Unionists really wanted Partition, why did it happen at all? This is a complicated story which you will investigate through the rest of this chapter, but here is a simplified picture of the main steps:

Step 1: The debate over Home Rule Nationalism and unionism became fixed on parallel tracks. They were two movements with incompatible aims: in other words, both sides could not get what they wanted. Pages 36–39 look at how this happened.

↓

Step 2: Armed conflict See pages 44–47.

↓

Step 3: Partition The British government lost the will to fight to keep Ireland united under British rule. It forced a compromise on the two reluctant sides.

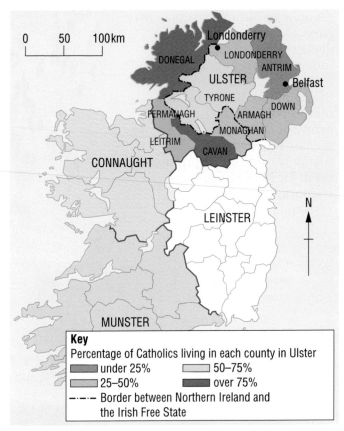

SOURCE 5 The results of the Anglo–Irish Treaty, 1922

SOURCE 6 A cartoon from *Punch*, 1922. In this cartoon David Lloyd George, the British Prime Minister, is unveiling Partition, his solution to the conflict in Ireland

Why were Nationalists and Unionists on the verge of civil war by 1914?

The Irish famine, 1845–51

From 1845 to 1851, Ireland suffered a traumatic famine. A disease called blight destroyed a large part of the potato crop in Ireland. Potatoes were the main food source for many people. The results were catastrophic in virtually all rural areas of Ireland, especially in the west.

Huge efforts to provide relief were made by local charities, including Protestant and Catholic churches. The British government's aid was ineffective. It was ignorant of the size of the Irish population and the massive scale of the disaster. Just as in England, it only offered relief in return for work, which most people were too weak to carry out. Over a million Irish people died from starvation and disease, while another million emigrated, mostly to the USA.

Many Nationalists saw the famine as proof of the failure of the Union as a way to govern Ireland. Bitter Irish emigrants in America became powerful supporters of movements opposed to British rule in Ireland.

The growth of nationalism

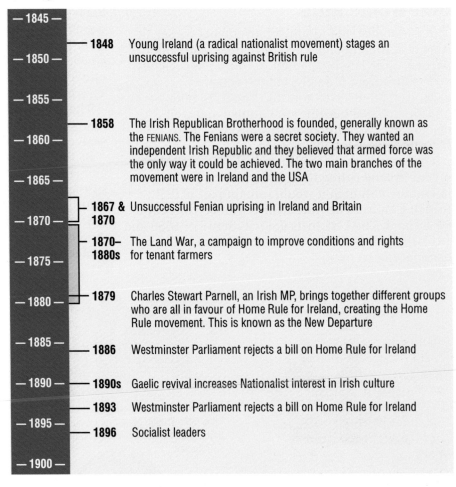

1848	Young Ireland (a radical nationalist movement) stages an unsuccessful uprising against British rule
1858	The Irish Republican Brotherhood is founded, generally known as the FENIANS. The Fenians were a secret society. They wanted an independent Irish Republic and they believed that armed force was the only way it could be achieved. The two main branches of the movement were in Ireland and the USA
1867 & 1870	Unsuccessful Fenian uprising in Ireland and Britain
1870– 1880s	The Land War, a campaign to improve conditions and rights for tenant farmers
1879	Charles Stewart Parnell, an Irish MP, brings together different groups who are all in favour of Home Rule for Ireland, creating the Home Rule movement. This is known as the New Departure
1886	Westminster Parliament rejects a bill on Home Rule for Ireland
1890s	Gaelic revival increases Nationalist interest in Irish culture
1893	Westminster Parliament rejects a bill on Home Rule for Ireland
1896	Socialist leaders

■ TASK

Over the next five pages you are going to examine a series of events which led Ireland to the verge of civil war between Unionists and Nationalists. This was a complicated period. There are many important events which could claim to be *the* decisive factor. Here are some of them.

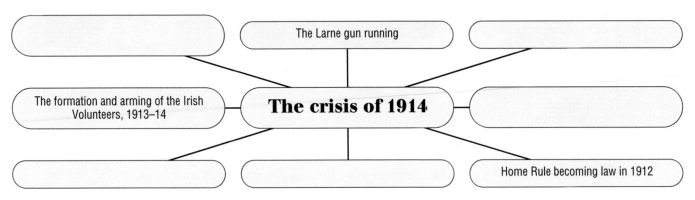

The Larne gun running

The formation and arming of the Irish Volunteers, 1913–14

The crisis of 1914

Home Rule becoming law in 1912

Over the next five pages you will complete this diagram, and then on page 41 you will analyse the importance of these factors.

Nationalists and Unionists divide over Home Rule

The nationalist and unionist movements we see in Northern Ireland today first developed into political parties in the late nineteenth century. Their beliefs and values were not new, but the way they organised themselves was. By the 1880s, both movements had become well funded and well disciplined. Most importantly, however, their objectives were totally opposed.

The critical issue was Home Rule. Home Rule meant Ireland ruling itself from its own parliament in Dublin, although it would remain part of the British Empire. The Nationalists wanted Home Rule for Ireland. The Unionists did not. Between 1880 and 1914, they moved from simply arguing about it to being prepared to fight.

The New Departure

Early attempts by Nationalists to oppose British rule were harmed because the nationalist movement was split. Then, in the 1880s, the nationalist leader Charles Stewart Parnell united some very different groups under his own leadership in the Home Rule Party. This policy became known as the New Departure.

The groups brought together by Parnell included many who had previously been very distrustful of each other. The diagram below shows who they were.

By the 1880s, the nationalist movement was strong and confident, well organised and well funded. A substantial amount of its funds came from Irish Americans who had emigrated to the USA in the years following the famine. It seemed very possible that the Nationalists' main aim of Home Rule would be achieved.

Most middle-class Catholics
They felt a Dublin parliament would offer them better opportunities in business, the civil service and the law.

A small number of Protestant landlords and professionals
They believed they would be key players in a Home Rule parliament. They also believed they could govern Ireland more effectively than a parliament in London.

The Fenians
Although they felt that Home Rule did not go far enough, they were prepared to support it as a step in the right direction.

Tenant farmers
As President of the Land League, Parnell supported the campaign for laws to protect tenants against their landlords and to help them buy the farms they worked.

Parnell

The Roman Catholic Church
Catholic bishops supported Home Rule because they felt the Church would have lots of influence on an Irish parliament.

SOURCE 1 Tim Healy, writing in the nationalist newspaper the *People's Advocate*, 1883

❝ *We must pave the way for Ireland to take her place among the nations of the earth. None of us whether in America or Ireland will be satisfied until we have destroyed the last link, which keeps Ireland bound to England.* ❞

Unionism and Home Rule

The unionist community in Ireland looked on with increasing concern at the rise of the nationalist movement in the 1880s. The rise of nationalism in turn strengthened unionism.

The Unionists were mainly Protestants, although there certainly were Catholic Unionists. Outside Ulster, most Unionists were Anglican Protestants. They were generally landowners or professionals (lawyers, doctors, etc). In Ulster, the main support for unionism came from the Presbyterian and Anglican (Church of Ireland) farming and business communities in Belfast and north-east Ulster. Unionists opposed Home Rule for different reasons, as this diagram shows.

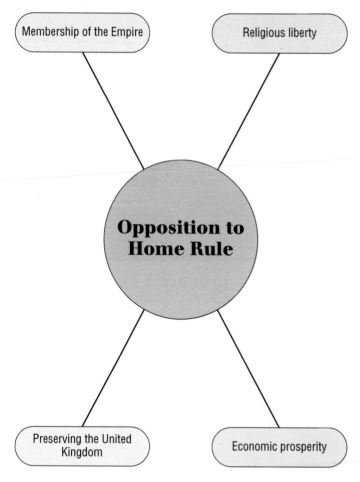

There were tensions within unionism. Moderate Unionists felt that support for nationalism was the result of poverty and economic backwardness in the rural parts of Ireland. They thought economic reform and development was the best way to defeat Home Rule. Hardline Unionists saw Home Rule as simply a Catholic plot, and total resistance as the only possible policy.

SOURCE 2 A statement by the Irish Loyal and Patriotic Union, a unionist campaign group opposed to Home Rule, 1886

66 *... the Irish people are at this moment very far in advance of the condition of their ancestors at the time of the Union. They are better housed, better clothed, better fed; they receive better prices for the produce of their farms, and higher wages for their labour; they have greater liberty and better protection in health, abundant provision for sickness, and facilities for the education and advancement in life of their children, such as were undreamt-of 80 years ago.* 99

Despite their divisions, all Unionists opposed Home Rule, and they did so with great success. Most importantly, they had the backing of many important politicians in mainland Britain, and most ordinary people as well (partly because of a strong anti-Catholic feeling at the time). The British opposed Home Rule because trade between Ireland and Britain was valuable. The greatest fear, however, was about the message Home Rule for Ireland would send to other parts of Britain's vast worldwide empire. In particular, if Ireland gained Home Rule, then India, Britain's most valuable possession by far, might follow suit.

Attempts to win Home Rule were defeated in 1886 and 1893. The Unionists seemed to be on top, but the Home Rule struggle divided the country, and few people thought of themselves as neutral. This issue would return to haunt Ireland.

■ TASK

1. Draw up a table like this to compare nineteenth-century nationalism and unionism.

	Nationalists	**Unionists**
Aims		
Supporters		
Strengths		
Weaknesses		
Divisions		

2. You have been commissioned to produce a leaflet for either the *People's Advocate* (Source 1) or the Irish Loyal and Patriotic Union (Source 2). They want five words on the front cover to summarise what the rest of the leaflet will say. What five words would you use?

The Home Rule crisis, 1912–14

Redmond revives the Nationalists

In the late nineteenth and early twentieth centuries, nationalism was changing. After the disappointments of 1886 and 1893 over Home Rule, radical nationalism was boosted by movements such as the Gaelic revival and SOCIALISM (see page 42). John Redmond also brought new life to the more moderate part of the nationalist movement. His Irish Parliamentary Party (IPP) regularly won over 80 seats in the Westminster Parliament. In 1910, Redmond got the chance he had been waiting for. The Liberal government needed the votes of Redmond's 82 MPs to pass the laws it wanted. In return for Redmond's support, the Liberals agreed to grant Home Rule to Ireland. It became law in 1912. However, the Unionists would not accept this.

Carson and Craig organise the Unionists

Edward Carson, a powerful Irish Conservative MP (see Source 3), led the unionist opposition. He was a strong speaker and an inspirational leader. He based his campaign in the unionist stronghold of Ulster, but he was determined that no part of Ireland should have Home Rule. He put forward both the economic arguments against Home Rule and the concerns about the Empire. However, more than anyone else he stressed the idea that Home Rule meant 'Rome Rule'. In other words, Home Rule was a Catholic movement. It threatened Ulster people's identity and their Protestant way of life. Ulster Unionists rallied to Carson in huge numbers.

SOURCE 3 A statue of Sir Edward Carson outside Stormont Castle, the home of the Northern Ireland government in Belfast. Carson is a hero for many people in the Protestant community in Northern Ireland for his leadership of the resistance to Home Rule in the period 1910–14

SOURCE 4 A unionist postcard from 1912 suggesting what would happen to Belfast under Home Rule

SOURCE 5 Sir Edward Carson signing the Ulster Solemn League and Covenant. This was a document promising to oppose Home Rule. Almost 500,000 men and women signed the document

Carson worked closely with James Craig, a Unionist MP, and together they were a formidable partnership. Craig was not inspirational like Carson, but he was more practical. He had doubts about whether all of Ireland could be kept in the Union, so he concentrated his efforts on preserving a Protestant Ulster. He made the Unionists into a well-organised and disciplined force.

Throughout 1912, Ulster Unionists held huge rallies protesting against Home Rule. They made it clear that they would form their own government in Ulster and use armed force to resist Home Rule. The Liberal Prime Minister, Asquith, assumed that the Unionists were bluffing, which only made the situation worse. The Nationalist leader, Redmond, also believed that the Unionists would back down (see Source 6). He thought the fact that a 'home ruled' Ireland would remain part of the British Empire would reassure most Unionists. However, he proved to be wrong.

THE ORANGEMAN'S ATTITUDE

CATHOLIC EMANCIPATION BILL

IRISH DISESTABLISHMENT BILL

HOME RULE BILL

"If you give Catholic Emancipation we shall revolt!" (*But they didn't!*)

"It you disestablish the Irish Church we shall revolt!" (*But they didn't!*)

"If you give Ireland Home Rule we shall revolt!" (*But they won't!*)

SOURCE 6 A cartoon from the nationalist Irish–American paper the *Irish World*, May 1912. 'Catholic Emancipation' refers to the removal, in 1829, of laws which had barred Catholics from important jobs such as the law, or from becoming MPs. 'Irish Disestablishment', which took place in 1869, meant that the Protestant Church of Ireland was no longer the official Church of the country

Why did Irish nationalism become more radical during 1916–21?

PUT YOURSELF IN the shoes of a Nationalist. The panels below show what has happened over the past 30 years.

By 1916, moderate Nationalists were still the vast majority, but they no longer held the initiative. The hardline Nationalists were increasingly strong. In their eyes, the path of moderation had failed. All that the attempts to achieve Home Rule had done was strengthen the Unionists. Coupled with this, the Gaelic revival and the socialist movement had strengthened the nationalist movement, and given the radicals opportunities to recruit others to their cause.

The factors that were making Nationalists more radical are summarised on these two pages.

The Gaelic revival

The period 1890–1916 saw many Irish people take an increasing interest in Irish history, language and culture. They felt that British rule was trying to wipe out all traces of Irish culture. This led to a Gaelic revival.

■ The Gaelic League published English and Irish works, old and new. It also ran classes in the Irish language.
■ The Gaelic Athletic Association re-established traditional sports such as Gaelic football and hurling.
■ These were not political organisations, but they were often the place where more extreme Nationalists met and recruited new members.

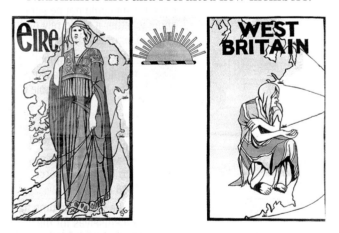

SOURCE 1 Eire (Ireland) contrasted with 'West Britain': a postcard by the Gaelic League in the early 1900s. In Northern Ireland and the Republic today, Nationalists who are thought to be too pro-British are sometimes called 'West Brits'

Socialism

During the same period, working-class movements (such as trade unions and the Labour Party) were growing in both Britain and Ireland.

The socialist movement was strongly linked to nationalism. James Connolly was one of the most important socialist leaders. He believed that a fair, socialist society could not be established in Ireland until Ireland was an independent state. He is still a much-admired figure in the republican movement, with many murals in Northern Ireland featuring him and his ideas.

SOURCE 2 An extract from the Irish Socialist Republican Party Manifesto, written by Connolly in 1896

66 The struggle for Irish freedom has two aspects: it is national and it is social. Its national ideal can never be realised until Ireland stands forth before the world a nation free and independent. It is social and economic, because no matter what the form of government may be, as long as one class owns as their private property the land and instruments of labour, from which all mankind derive their substance, that class will always have it in their power to plunder and enslave the remainder of their fellow creatures. 99

Bitter disputes taking place in all parts of Britain at this time included a vicious dock strike in Dublin in 1913. James Connolly created an Irish Citizen Army to protect strikers and demonstrators in the regular street battles with police.

1. The artist in Source 1 is trying to say that Ireland would be better off as an independent Eire than as 'West Britain', a province of the United Kingdom. How does the source try to get this message across?

Unionist radicalism

You have read about Unionist actions between 1912–14. These events seemed to show that radical action and the threat of violence worked.

Revival of the Irish Republican Brotherhood

The IRB was formed in the mid-nineteenth century. It had two branches. The Irish branch, set up in 1848, was headed by James Stephens. The American wing was known as the Fenians, and by the 1860s both branches of the IRB were often referred to as Fenians. The IRB aimed to set up an independent Irish republic by force of arms. This was because they believed Britain would never agree to an independent Ireland any other way. IRB members worked in a variety of ways.

In the early twentieth century, radical Nationalists such as Thomas Clarke, Padraig Pearse, Sean MacDermott and Eamon de Valera breathed new life into the Irish Republican Brotherhood (IRB). They admired the achievements of Parnell and were inspired by Ireland's history, especially by past Irish revolutionaries such as Wolfe Tone. Their view of history was often selective (see Source 3). In this history, of course, everything about the British connection was bad for Ireland. Many IRB members also belonged to Sinn Fein (see right). They infiltrated the Gaelic League's cultural and sporting organisations. They also infiltrated the Volunteers, creating a force within a force.

> SOURCE 3 Dan Breen, a leading IRB man and later an important politician in Ireland, describing his education
>
> 66 He [the teacher] did not confine his history lesson to the official textbook. He gave us the naked facts about the English conquest of Ireland and the manner in which our country was held in bondage. We learned about the Penal Laws, the systematic ruining of Irish trade, the elimination of our native language. He also told us of the ruthless manner in which Irish rebellions had been crushed. By the time we had passed from his class, we were no longer content to grow up 'happy English children' as envisaged by the Board of Education. 99

2. Would you regard Source 3 as an example of history being used selectively? Explain your answer.

Sinn Fein

Sinn Fein was founded in 1905 by Arthur Griffith as a more radical rival to John Redmond's moderate nationalist party, the IPP. *Sinn Fein* is Gaelic, and can be translated as 'We Ourselves', or 'Ourselves Alone'. Griffith believed that all Irish MPs should withdraw from Westminster. He thought that they should set up their own parliament in Dublin. In by-elections and general elections up to 1910, Sinn Fein achieved little.

However, as tension increased over the Home Rule crisis, support for Sinn Fein began to increase as well. Griffith set out a vision of an independent Ireland, with its own government determining Ireland's social and economic policies on key issues like land and religion. Younger Nationalists began to feel that Sinn Fein's more radical approach would be more effective than Redmond's MPs in London in achieving Home Rule.

The new generation of hardline Irish Nationalists were no longer content with Home Rule. They wanted complete separation of the whole of Ireland from Britain. They also wanted nothing to do with the Empire. They wanted an Irish Republic.

■ ACTIVITY

As you consider the events of the next five years, you are going to try to see them through the eyes of a moderate Nationalist. Moderates formed the majority of the movement. At various points you will be given options to choose between, and you must explain your choice.

Here is your starter.

Decision point 1: Redmond or Sinn Fein, 1910
You are the son or daughter of moderate nationalist parents. Your parents supported Parnell and are now firm supporters of Redmond. You are trying to decide who you will give your support to. Your family argue strongly that the future lies with Redmond. However, some friends find the radical groups – Sinn Fein or even the IRB – more attractive.

Will you support Redmond or will you support Sinn Fein? Write a paragraph to explain your decision. Include an explanation of why you have rejected the other options.

The Easter Rising, 1916

By the spring of 1916, leading IRB figures were concerned that the issue of Ireland's freedom was being ignored because of the First World War. They decided that armed action would put life back into the nationalist movement. The exact aims of the Easter Rising are unclear. Some accounts suggest that its leader, Padraig Pearse, saw the rebellion as a 'blood sacrifice'. In other words, he knew the rising was hopeless, but he feared that without some action the flame of nationalism would go out in Ireland. This theory is controversial for several reasons. Firstly, the original plan was that the rebellion should involve a much larger force than the rebels eventually ended up with. Secondly, Pearse was allied with much more practical men such as James Connolly, who would not have supported the rising if they thought it had no chance of success.

On Easter Monday 1916, about 1200 IRB Volunteers and James Connolly's Citizen Army members occupied parts of central Dublin. On the first day of the rising, Pearse read out a proclamation declaring that the Irish Republic was now established (Source 5). It was a momentous event in Ireland's history.

SOURCE 5 Proclamation of the Irish Republic, 1916. The document is kept in the National Museum of Ireland in Dublin today

SOURCE 4 Extracts from the diary of Alfred Fannin, 1916. Fannin was not involved in the rising. He was a wealthy businessman who lived in Dublin and observed the events going on around him

66 *Tuesday, April 25th*
Yesterday, Easter Monday, the Sinn Feiners tried to occupy all the railway stations – some successfully, others not – the GPO, Jacob's factory and St Stephen's Green. They barricaded all the doors, and fired on anyone in uniform who approached. They have blocked the roads to St Stephen's Green, and while they allow civilians to walk about, they are shooting at anyone they see in khaki.
. . . A great deal of the shooting is aimless. There is now a barricade of motor cars across the road opposite Russell's Hotel . . . The College of Surgeons is held by the rebels with a republican flag over it.

Wednesday, April 26th
After breakfast we heard that St Stephen's Green was now in the hands of the military. Later the rumours in the road were first that the GPO had been taken by the military, second that it had not.
. . . It was too dangerous to go out . . . We used to think we were clear of the war here in Ireland but we have certainly got it close enough now.

Thursday, April 27th
I went down to the Morehampton Road shop. All there was normal but supplies somewhat limited . . . all meat was commandeered by the military. Carried home two stone of potatoes and meat, everybody was out carrying their own stores.

Friday, April 28th
Plenty of talk and rumours but no definite news . . . Grafton Street was absolutely deserted except for soldiers at regular intervals.

Saturday, April 29th
The GPO has been taken. The day wore slowly away and towards evening news came that the Sinn Feiners had made an unconditional surrender. This is, of course, provisionally speaking. The revolt is too widespread to be stopped in a minute but it gave some hope for a peaceful Sunday.

May 10th
We are still under martial law. There have been a good many executions and we must all be in at 8.30 at night, but the city by day is resuming its normal appearance. 99

The rising was short-lived. Just one week later, the rebels surrendered. The British people were outraged by the rebellion, in the middle of their own bitter war against Germany. The leaders of the rising were executed by the British government.

3. What does Fannin's account of the rising tell historians about
a) Fannin himself
b) life in Dublin during the rising
c) people's knowledge of the events going on around them?
4. Fannin was an eyewitness, and we usually think that an account from an eyewitness is a valuable source. How valuable is Fannin's account of the events of April 1916?

The traditional view of the events of 1916 is that most people in Ireland were totally opposed to the rebellion as it took place, but once the British started executing the rebel leaders, opinion in Ireland changed. More recently, the Irish historian J.J. Lee has questioned this. He argues that there may have been more support than at first thought. Certainly, the rising became part of the republican legend.

5. What do Sources 6 and 7 tell historians about the impact of the rising on support for the republican movement?
6. Explain why historians would find Sources 5, 6 and 7 more helpful when used together than used separately.

SOURCE 6 Part of a letter written by A. Bonaparte-Wyse, a hardline Unionist working in the British civil service in Ireland. He later became a senior civil servant in Northern Ireland. The Easter Rising was not organised by Sinn Fein, but most people at the time assumed it was

66 *The city is quiet now, but there is a very menacing tone among the lower classes who openly praise the Sinn Feiners for their courage and bravery, and there is a lot of abuse of the soldiers. . . . The sympathies of the ordinary Irish are with Sinn Fein. They want independence and their only criticism of the rebellion is that it was foolish (not criminal or otherwise wrong), but just foolish because it had no chance of success.* 99

■ **ACTIVITY**

Decision point 2: the Easter Rising of 1916
Look back at your work for the Activity on page 43, when you were thinking about how you, as a young moderate, would decide whether to support the Nationalists or Sinn Fein.

1. How do you think you would have reacted to:

■ the outbreak of the Easter Rising
■ Pearse's Proclamation of the Irish Republic
■ Pearse's surrender
■ the executions which followed the rising?

2. How might your reaction to the rising compare with the reaction of:

■ the mainly unionist press
■ your parents?

3. In the wake of the Easter Rising, would you:

■ support the Nationalists under Redmond
■ support or join Sinn Fein
■ support or join the IRB?

Once again, explain your decisions and explain why you have rejected the other options.

SOURCE 7 An American print showing the execution of James Connolly. Connolly was the last rebel to be executed. He was wounded in the leg in the fighting. The wound became infected with gangrene and he was already dying when he was executed. This execution generated more anti-British feeling than any other

The rise of Sinn Fein

The Easter Rising and the execution of its leaders boosted support for Sinn Fein.

The real breakthrough for Sinn Fein came early in 1918. As the First World War was still raging the British government considered introducing conscription (compulsory military service) to Ireland. The Irish Parliamentary Party (IPP) and Sinn Fein protested successfully against this measure, but Sinn Fein gained most of the credit. In the Westminster Parliament elections of December 1918, they swept the IPP away. The results were as follows:

- Sinn Fein 73 seats
- Unionists 26 seats
- IPP 6 seats.

7. What does Source 8 suggest about nationalist attitudes to British rule in Ireland?

8. What does the cartoon suggest about Sinn Fein's methods?

SOURCE 8 A postcard issued by Sinn Fein after the election in 1918

SOURCE 9 Eamon de Valera writing in May 1921

66 *I do not see any hope of ending the struggle with England through a prior agreement with the unionist minority. At the bottom the question is an Irish–English one, and the solution must be sought in the larger general picture of English politics.* 99

In 1919, Sinn Fein MPs declared themselves to be DAIL EIREANN, the government of Ireland. The Dail (pronounced 'Doyl') set up an administrative system, police and courts. It simply ignored British institutions and officials. The Volunteers and the IRB became the Irish Republican Army (IRA).

In many areas the Dail was viewed as the official government. However, in Ulster loyalty to the British Crown remained strong.

The British Prime Minister, Lloyd George, viewed the rise of the radical Nationalists with alarm. So did Unionists in Ulster. Sinn Fein leader Eamon de Valera wanted the entire island of Ireland to become an independent Irish state for the Irish people. De Valera was a devout Roman Catholic and also a Gaelic League enthusiast. To Unionists, it looked as though only Irish-speaking Catholics from a Celtic Irish background would be welcome in de Valera's Ireland.

De Valera and other members of Sinn Fein did little to calm Unionist fears. In fact, they did not really seem to take account of them at all (see Source 9). De Valera believed that Britain was using the Unionists as an excuse to block Irish independence. He thought that if Sinn Fein could make the British withdraw, the Unionists would accept an independent Ireland.

9. Write a list of short sentences to explain why Unionists in Ulster would have been concerned about the rise of Sinn Fein.

■ ACTIVITY A

Decision point 3: 1919
How do you think you, as a young moderate Nationalist, would respond to: the Sinn Fein election victory? The formation of the Dail? The setting up of Dail courts and other governmental systems?

Would you:

- support the Nationalists under Redmond
- support or join Sinn Fein
- support or join the IRB?

The Anglo–Irish War, 1919–21

The IRA began a bitter guerrilla war against the Royal Irish Constabulary. The IRA attacked the RIC for several reasons: to gain arms (the RIC's own weapons, or weapons and explosives the RIC were guarding); to discourage any form of collaboration with the British (most RIC officers were local Irish Catholics but the IRA saw them as collaborators); and to destroy the British intelligence network. Britain sent in troops, including new forces called the BLACK AND TANS, to defeat the IRA, but its leader Michael Collins organised his small forces well. Local IRA commanders organised their men in flying columns, which carried out hit-and-run raids. They then hid their weapons and blended back among the ordinary people. One of the most famous (and ruthless) IRA commanders was Tom Barry, a former British Army soldier. His West Cork Flying Column managed to stay active despite facing over 10,000 British troops and police in his area.

SOURCE 10 Eamon de Valera writing in 1937, from the preface to a history book called *The Irish Republic*

66 No matter what the future may hold for the Irish nation, the seven years – 1916 to 1923 – must ever remain a period of absorbing interest.

Not for over 200 years has there been such a period of intense and sustained effort to regain the national sovereignty and independence. Over the greater part of the period it was the effort of, one might say, the entire nation. An overwhelming majority of the people of this island combined voluntarily during these years in pursuit of a common purpose.

There was a wonderful unanimity, and the great movement of Sinn Fein, of which a British intelligence officer wrote that it had 'worked together with greater devotion than any other coalition recorded in history'. 99

10. According to de Valera (Source 10), did Sinn Fein and the IRA have the support of the people?
11. Explain why a historian might want to check de Valera's account of the period of 1916–23 against other evidence.

Both sides committed appalling acts. The Black and Tans burned homes, and killed and tortured IRA suspects and innocent civilians. Collins was utterly ruthless, for example, he had an elderly government accountant, Alan Bell, assassinated, because he was getting close to locating some IRA funds. The IRA killed Protestant farmers, especially in the areas on the border between Ulster and the rest of Ireland.

SOURCE 11 An extract from *Ireland, the 20th Century* by Charles Townshend, a leading authority on the Anglo–Irish War

66 The republican publicity organisation which formed an integral part of the Dail government was extremely effective in building up a picture of full-scale national mobilisation behind the Dail and the IRA. The litany of British atrocities described in the Irish Bulletin ... helped to convince public opinion in countries like France and the USA, and to some extent even in Britain, that Irish resistance was unanimous. The Bulletin was a great propaganda triumph, but modern historians have been more sceptical of the image projected. While the IRA certainly could not have operated as effectively as it did if the Irish public had been hostile, the rebels themselves were acutely conscious of widespread indifference. 99

IRA attacks in Ulster were followed by loyalist REPRISALS. Catholic homes and businesses were destroyed by loyalist mobs. In Ulster, around 500 people – Catholics, Protestants and police – were killed in various riots, attacks and battles between 1920 and 1922. Some 11,000 Catholics were driven out of their jobs.

By 1921, the war had reached stalemate. Divisions were emerging among the Nationalists. The Irish people were fed up with conflict and the British government was very sensitive to criticisms of its policy at home and abroad (see Source 11).

■ ACTIVITY B

Decision point 4: atrocities, 1921

Look back at previous decisions you have made, as a young moderate, in this enquiry. You have just heard about some of the atrocities committed by both sides in the war. How would you react to this? Would you:

■ blame the British because of the atrocities they have committed
■ support the IRA because they were only doing what they had to do
■ wonder whether your cause was really worth all the suffering and bloodshed?

Why did the British government partition Ireland?

PARTITION WAS NOT really an event, it was a process which took place between 1920 and 1922. For decades, the British had resisted Home Rule, but by 1919 attitudes were shifting. To many British people, the issue seemed less important after the devastation they had lived through during the First World War (see Source 1). Three great empires – Russia, Austria–Hungary and Germany – had fallen in the Great War. The politicians of the world were trying to create lasting peace. Conflict in Ireland seemed unimportant in this context.

Lloyd George's problems

When the IRA began its guerrilla war in 1919, the British Prime Minister, Lloyd George, was involved in the Paris Peace Conference, redrawing the map of Europe and the world after the First World War. Later in 1919, he turned his attention to Ireland. He had some sympathy for Irish nationalism, but he had no time for violence and law-breaking, so he sent extra troops to Ireland. He planned to crush the IRA, reach an acceptable deal with the Unionists and then talk to Sinn Fein about a settlement. However, this was not as simple as it seemed.

Firstly, it is very hard to win a guerrilla war, and the British troops could not defeat the IRA. Secondly, Lloyd George could not impose a settlement on the Unionists. He relied on Unionist supporters to keep his position as Prime Minister.

SOURCE 1 Part of a speech by the British politician Winston Churchill in Parliament in 1919. He was comparing the First World War to a flood which had swept away most of the old world

66 *The whole map of Europe has been changed. The position of countries has been violently altered. The way men think, the whole outlook on affairs, the grouping of parties, all have gone through violent and tremendous changes in this war. But as the flood subsides and the waters fall we see the dreary steeples of Fermanagh and Tyrone emerging once again. The Irish quarrel is one of the few institutions that has been unaltered in the disaster which has swept the world.* 99

Lloyd George's compromise: the Government of Ireland Act

In December 1920, Lloyd George introduced the Government of Ireland Act. This had three main terms:

- Six of Ulster's nine counties became a self-governing Northern Ireland, with its own parliament in Belfast.
- The remaining 26 counties would also become self-governing with a parliament in Dublin.
- Britain would keep control of issues such as the military, naval facilities, and so on.

Unionist reaction

The Unionists reluctantly accepted this Act. It was a disappointment to them that the whole island of Ireland would not remain part of the United Kingdom. But they knew they were losing sympathy in Britain. They were also concerned that a future London government might betray them and give in to the Nationalists. This plan for a Northern Ireland parliament put their future in their own hands, rather than in the hands of politicians in London.

Where should the border go?

The main issue for the Unionists was which counties would be in the new state of Northern Ireland.

Many Unionists wanted it to be all nine counties of the province of Ulster. However, this would have created a state where the nationalist and unionist populations were finely balanced, without a clear unionist majority.

Another option was for the new Northern Ireland to consist of only the four counties where there was a clear unionist majority. However, it was felt this would be too small to work economically, as the state might not be able to feed itself, and might not have enough workers for its industries.

In the end, James Craig as the leader of the Unionists insisted that Northern Ireland would be six counties (see Source 4 on page 34). This meant a unionist majority of about 65 per cent, to 35 per cent Nationalists.

The Government of Ireland Act came into effect in May 1921, and Craig became Northern Ireland's first Prime Minister. It was a compromise which at the time appeared to guarantee Northern Ireland's security. With hindsight, we see it differently.

The Anglo–Irish Treaty

In the rest of Ireland, Sinn Fein rejected the Act and the war continued.

By the summer of 1921, Lloyd George was desperate to find an end to the Irish conflict. There were several reasons for this:

■ He had many other concerns, with economic and industrial problems at home.
■ He was anxious to try to rebuild Britain's international trade, which had been badly damaged in the war. He could not afford the 100,000 troops and £100 million which his military advisers said he needed in order to crush the IRA.
■ He was being heavily criticised at home and abroad, especially by the USA, for British tactics in Ireland (see Source 3).
■ Britain had gone to war in 1914 to defend the rights of small nations like Belgium, and yet it seemed that Ireland was being denied these rights.

The two sides called a truce in July 1921. Negotiations began in October. The Republicans were deeply divided, and they were also up against some of the most able politicians of the period. The negotiations were watched anxiously in Ireland. Nationalists hoped for peace and independence. Unionists in Northern Ireland feared that Lloyd George might betray their new state to the Sinn Feiners.

The terms

The final terms of the Anglo–Irish treaty built on the Government of Ireland Act:

■ The 26 counties of Ireland would become the Irish Free State, with its own administration.
■ All British forces were to leave the 26 counties.
■ The Free State would have its own army and police; coinage and stamps; flag and passports.
■ The Republicans must accept Partition and the existence of Northern Ireland. However, a Boundary Commission would decide exactly where the border between Northern Ireland and the Free State should be. This would go a long way towards solving the problem of the nationalist minority in Northern Ireland.
■ The Free State was still technically part of the British Empire.
■ Politicians in the Free State Parliament, the Dail, had to swear an oath of allegiance to the British monarch.
■ The Royal Navy could still use the Irish ports of Cobh, Brerehaven and Lough Swilly.

For the great majority, the treaty was good enough, because it brought the hope of peace. In June 1922, the people of the Free State voted decisively in favour of the treaty. The hardline Republicans led by Eamon de Valera, on the other hand, were deeply disappointed by the last four terms and refused to accept them. Anti-treaty members of the IRA went even further, and within a short time the Free State was involved in a bitter civil war which lasted until May 1923. Many Nationalists in Northern Ireland were dismayed by the treaty. They felt that they had been abandoned by the Republican leaders. However, they were hopeful that the Boundary Commission would resolve many problems.

The Boundary Commission reported in 1924, at a time when the Free State was in no position to take a strong stand against it. The Commission made virtually no changes to the proposed border between Northern Ireland and the Free State. Ireland was divided. The questions now were: could the two states exist as neighbours? and could Northern Ireland cope with its internal divisions?

FREE STATE OF IRELAND.

ARTICLES OF HISTORIC AGREEMENT.

A RELATIONSHIP THE SAME AS WITH CANADA.

"ULSTER" GETS A MONTH TO SAY IF SHE WILL STAY IN.

IRISH PROVISIONAL GOVERNMENT AT ONCE.

SOURCE 2 Reconstructed newspaper headlines of 7–8 December, 1921, showing how news of the treaty was reported

SOURCE 3 A cartoon from December 1920 which appeared in the English newspaper the *Star*. The Prime Minister, David Lloyd George, was a fierce critic of the IRA's guerrilla tactics. The cartoonist, David Low, was a political radical who attacked any policies he saw as unfair, no matter who the politician was

"Were Not We, Too?"

[The forces of law and order were entitled to the support of every honest citizen, Liberal as well as Conservative, for we were all under the same protection. (Cheers.)"— MR. LLOYD GEORGE at the Conservative Club

■ REVIEW TASK

Look back at all your work in this chapter. In pairs or groups, decide which of the following views is best supported by the evidence.

a) The Unionists' determination to resist Home Rule meant that by 1922 Partition was the only realistic solution.

b) The Nationalists' determination to have either Home Rule or a Republic meant that by 1922 Partition was the only realistic solution.

c) Britain was anxious to end conflict in Ireland in 1922 and Partition offered the only instant solution.

d) The combination of two or more factors explains why Ireland was divided in 1922.

You may find it helpful to use a table like this one to help you record your decisions.

View	Evidence which supports it	Reason

chapter 4

HOW PEACEFUL WAS NORTHERN IRELAND IN 1922–68?

> 66 *She said to me 'Why is a young man like you concerned about Northern Ireland? What about Vietnam? What about Rhodesia?' I just said, 'You'll see when they start shooting one another.'* 99

Fast track: From Partition to civil rights – Northern Ireland, 1922–68

PARTITION CREATED THE new state of Northern Ireland (see Source 1). This was a compromise. It was not the ideal solution for anyone. This meant that whether Northern Ireland would flourish and develop as a peaceful country largely depended on how far its citizens were prepared to compromise and work together. For example:

■ Would the nationalist minority (a third of the population) accept the existence of the new state and work for its success?
■ Would the unionist majority (the other two thirds) govern fairly and work for the good of both communities?
■ Would both communities try to learn about each other's hopes and fears, and compromise where necessary?

In this chapter, you will investigate how the people of Northern Ireland responded to this challenge, but first here is an overview of the main events you will be investigating.

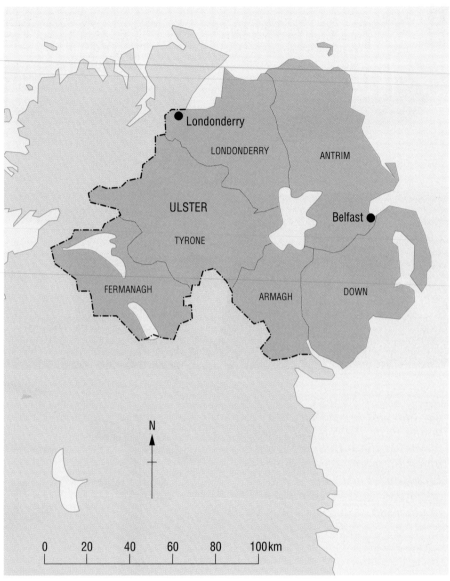

SOURCE 1 The new state of Northern Ireland after the Boundary Commission report of 1923

■ ACTIVITY

Look at the overview of events in Northern Ireland's history, 1922–68, in Source 2. In pairs or groups, make a list of:

■ events or developments which seem to increase tension
■ events or developments which seem to reduce tension.

Compare your findings with those of other students in your class. At this stage you are only basing your judgements on a broad outline of events. When you have finished your work on the rest of this chapter look back and see if your views have changed.

Prime Minister of Northern Ireland	Northern Ireland society		Factors affecting relationship with 'the South'	'The South' known as …
	Throughout this period most of population live normal lives, but Protestants and Catholics are segregated	**1920**	Throughout this period UK government largely ignores internal politics in Northern Ireland	
	1920s Many Catholics rejected the State of Northern Ireland Discrimination against Catholics in areas such as politics and employment		**1920** Government of Ireland Act **1922** Anglo–Irish Treaty **1924** Boundary Commission fixes border	Irish Free State
Sir James Craig (later Lord Craigavon) **1922–40**	**1930s** Worldwide economic depression – Catholics and Protestants suffer	**1930**		
	Serious sectarian violence especially **1934–37** Unemployment and competition for jobs increase tension		Tension over policies of de Valera, especially over the **1937** Constitution **1939** Northern Ireland enters Second World War with rest of UK	
John Andrews **1940–43**		**1940**		Eire
			1939–1945 Eire remains neutral during war	
Basil Brooke (later Lord Brookeborough) **1943–63**	**1948–1950s** Protestants and Catholics share the benefits and prosperity brought by the introduction of the Welfare State	**1950**	**1948** Introduction of Welfare State **1949** Remaining ties with Empire broken **1950s** Republic has one of the poorest economies in Europe	Republic of Ireland
	1956–1962 IRA campaign – lack of support from Northern Ireland's Catholic community a key factor	**1960**		
Terence O'Neill **1963–69**		**1970**		

SOURCE 2 Timeline 1920–70

Why did Partition not bring peace in the 1920s and 1930s?

SOURCES 1–7 SHOW OR describe Northern Ireland in the 1920s and 1930s.

■ TASK A

Work with a partner. Using Sources 1–7, draw up a list of problems facing Northern Ireland in the 1920s and 1930s.

SOURCE 1 Part of a speech by Sir Basil Brooke, a member of the Unionist government. He was later to become Prime Minister of Northern Ireland

66 There are a great number of Protestants and Orangemen who employ Catholics. I would point out that Roman Catholics are trying to get in everywhere … I would appeal to Loyalists, therefore, wherever possible, to employ Protestant lads and lassies. 99

SOURCE 2 Northern Ireland nationalist leader Joe Devlin complaining about the attitude of Unionist leaders and politicians in March 1932

66 You had opponents willing to co-operate. We did not seek office. We sought service. We were willing to help. But you rejected all friendly offers … You went on the old political lines, fostering hatreds, keeping one third of the population as if they were pariahs in the community. 99

SOURCE 3 Farm workers in Northern Ireland in 1948. Much of Northern Ireland's population worked on the land, growing food, or flax for the linen industry. Although historians tend to concentrate on the conflict in Northern Ireland, it is important to remember that the majority of people wanted only to live normal peaceful lives

SOURCE 4 The remains of a train blown up by the IRA near Newry, County Down, in 1921. IRA violence continued in Northern Ireland throughout the early years of the new state

SOURCE 5 A scene from the 1932 outdoor relief riots in Belfast. Unemployment reached very high levels during the worldwide economic depression of the 1930s. Disease and poverty were worse in Northern Ireland than in any other part of the United Kingdom, and unemployment benefit was the lowest. In 1932, unemployed Catholics and Protestants protested for higher benefits. When the police tried to stop them, they fought together against the police. In this picture the cobblestones have been pulled up for use as missiles against the police

SOURCE 6 A socialist speaker in Belfast in 1935. Labour leaders were often frustrated that they could not get Catholic and Protestant workers to unite against employers, even though Belfast had the lowest wages and standards of living of any British city in the 1930s. In this extract a human gull is someone who is gullible, or easily led

66 *If you took all the Orange sashes and all the Green sashes in Belfast and tied them round loaves of bread and threw them in the River Lagan, the gulls, the ordinary seagulls, would go for the bread, but the other gulls – like you – you'd go for the sashes every time.* 99

SOURCE 7 Comments by the Belfast City Coroner after riots that occurred in 1935 between Unionists and Nationalists

66 *It is all so wanton and meaningless ... The poor people who commit these riots are easily led and influenced ... there would be less bigotry if there was less public speechmaking of a kind by so-called leaders of public opinion ... It is not good Protestantism to preach a gospel of hate and enmity towards those who differ from us in religion and politics.* 99

1. Would you say that Source 7 is a criticism of the kind of views expressed in Source 1? Explain your answer.
2. What did the speaker in Source 6 mean by the phrase 'you'd go for the sashes every time'?

■ TASK B

The State of Northern Ireland was set up by the Government of Ireland Act 1920 (see page 48). The British government in London was ultimately responsible for the running of Northern Ireland. However, after Partition, the British government paid little or no attention to the Province.

The year is 1936, and you are the Belfast Coroner in Source 7. You are therefore a professional person, loyal to Northern Ireland but concerned about some of the things happening in it. Your task is to write a letter to the British government, criticising them for their lack of interest in the Province since Partition. You should explain:

■ what problems are troubling Northern Ireland. Use your findings from Task A to guide you
■ how the British government might have avoided some of these problems by acting as a mediator between the two communities in Northern Ireland.

You should also make the point that most people in Northern Ireland simply want to live normal peaceful lives.

Partition did not create a tranquil and problem-free Northern Ireland. For some people, life continued as normal, but for others there were major problems. There was serious tension during much of the 1920s and 1930s. The reasons for this are shown below.

IRA violence

In the early 1920s, the IRA conducted a violent campaign against the new state. The Unionist government suspected that the government in Dublin was supporting the IRA. IRA violence also made the government suspicious of its own nationalist population. It set up a special security force, the B-SPECIALS, to help the police deal with IRA violence.

Segregation

Segregation was a fact of life. Nationalists and Unionists went to separate churches and separate pubs. Even the workplace was often exclusively Protestant or exclusively Catholic. Education kept the country divided as well. In 1926, the senior Unionist minister Lord Londonderry tried to get Protestant and Catholic children educated together. He resigned when his plans were blocked by protests which were led by the Catholic Church and supported by Presbyterians.

Discrimination

Discrimination against Catholics became a feature of the Northern Ireland state, even at the highest levels. For example, Catholics rarely got jobs in the civil service. The Minister for Home Affairs, Richard Dawson Bates, refused to use his own telephone until a Catholic telephone operator in his department had been transferred to another post. Unionist leaders were also deeply suspicious of socialism. Some of their actions to reduce the threat of the labour movement (such as the abolition of PR) actually resulted in discrimination against Catholics.

Boycotts

In the early 1920s, many Nationalists were still hoping that the Boundary Commission (see page 49) would move the border so that they would live in the Free State. They did little to hide the fact that they did not wish to be part of Northern Ireland.

In the 1920 local council elections, the Nationalists gained majorities in Londonderry, Fermanagh and Tyrone. These councils refused to accept the authority of the new Belfast government when it was formally established in June 1922, and they only acknowledged the Dail. The Belfast government suspended and then dissolved the councils and appointed a government commissioner to take over the running of all services and functions of the councils.

Nationalist politicians refused to sit in Northern Ireland's parliament until 1926. They walked out again in 1932, when the Unionists scrapped PR.

Problems in Northern Ireland in the 1920s and 1930s

Economic problems

In the 1930s, the worldwide economic depression hit Northern Ireland hard. Protestants and Catholics were competing for scarce jobs and trade. This rivalry spilled over into sectarian tension and violence. There were particularly serious riots between the Nationalists and Unionists in 1934 and 1935 in Belfast, following on from Orange Order marches.

Election fixing

The CONSTITUTION specified that all elections would be by PROPORTIONAL REPRESENTATION (PR). The purpose of this was to give minority groups fair representation in Northern Ireland. In 1922, the Unionists abolished it for local elections. The British government made no protest against this action, even though it broke the terms of the Government of Ireland Act.

Nationalist MPs withdrew from the political process in protest at the decision to scrap PR. This made the problem worse, since they were not consulted when the boundaries of wards (areas which elected councillors) were redrawn. The result was GERRYMANDERING – fixing the boundaries so that the Unionists gained the results they wanted.

In 1929, the Unionist government also abolished PR in general elections. Once again, the Nationalists walked out in protest. The British government took no action.

Distrust

Partition created a large nationalist Catholic minority in Northern Ireland. This minority felt isolated in the new state when it was first formed. Unionists did not make much effort to build bridges with the Nationalists. There was distrust on both sides. The Unionists felt the Nationalists wanted to undermine the new state, while the Nationalists felt the Unionists wanted to exclude them from power.

The influence of the Free State

Events in the Free State increased tensions in Northern Ireland. In the 1920s, the Dail banned divorce and introduced censorship. This strengthened Protestant views that the Free State was a country dominated by a repressive Catholic Church. In the 1930s, Eamon de Valera became the head of the Free State government. He announced his plans for Ireland:

- a politically and economically independent Ireland
- a Gaelic Ireland which emphasised Irish language and culture
- a Catholic Ireland
- a united Ireland.

De Valera cut political links with Britain, and ignored the Governor General, the British monarch's representative in Ireland. He made the Irish language a key part of the education system. His policies triggered a trade war with Britain from 1933 to 1935, which brought great hardship to many people in his own country and in Northern Ireland.

In 1937, he unveiled a new constitution for the Free State, or Eire as it now became. Article 2 caused a particular outcry in Northern Ireland (see Source 8). Speeches by de Valera in 1937 and 1938 made it quite clear that he planned to press the British government to end Partition.

SOURCE 8 Extracts from the Constitution of Eire, 1937

66 *Article 2 The national territory consists of the whole island of Ireland, its islands and the territorial seas.*

Article 4 The name of the State is Eire, or, in the English language, Ireland.

Article 7 The national flag is the Tricolour of green, white and orange.

Article 8.1 The Irish language as the national language is the first official language.

Article 8.2 The English language is recognised as a second official language.

Article 41 The State recognises the Family as the natural primary and fundamental unit group of Society . . . guarantees to protect the Family welfare of the Nation and the State.
The State pledges itself to guard with special care the institution of Marriage, on which the Family is founded, and to protect it against attack. No law shall be enacted providing for the grant of a dissolution of marriage.

Article 44 The State recognises the special position of the Holy Catholic Apostolic and Roman Church as the guardian of the Faith professed by the great majority of the Citizens. 99

■ ACTIVITY A

Write a short article about the Constitution of 1937 for a unionist radio broadcast. Read Source 8. You should think carefully about how Northern Ireland Unionists would have felt about:

- Article 2
- Article 41
- Article 44.

You should also consider how the Constitution would affect attitudes towards Catholics in Northern Ireland.

■ ACTIVITY B

Why did Partition fail to end tensions in Northern Ireland in the 1920s and 1930s?

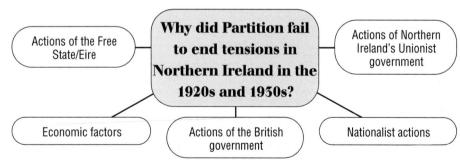

Make your own copy of this diagram.

1. For each category in the diagram, find one example from the last four pages of this factor increasing (or failing to end) tension.
2. Draw lines between any factors or examples which seem to be linked.
3. Compare your diagram with someone else's. Discuss whether you think one factor is more important than any other.

How was sectarian tension reduced in the 1950s and 1960s?

SOURCES 1 AND 2 describe two Belfast communities in the 1950s and 1960s. What impression do they give you of sectarian tension?

> **SOURCE 1** Extract from *The Passion of Peace*, the autobiography of the Catholic peace campaigner Ciaran McKeown, published in 1984. He is writing about the period 1955–63

66 ... *where we lived, we were divided equally, one half of the street for Northern Ireland people (mainly Protestant), the other half for engineers and designers from the mainland to work in the new aircraft and missile factory of Short Brothers and Harland.*

I can recall only about three examples of sectarianism. Shortly after we came to Belfast, a neighbour's children used to throw stones at us McKeowns, shouting 'Fenians' at us. Our parents told us to take no notice, vaguely explaining that these neighbours came from an area where that kind of behaviour was not uncommon.

It turned out that the neighbour was from the loyalist Shankill Road area, and had been shipwrecked during the war: his behaviour was put down to 'war nerves'. I remember an Englishman ticking him off for being rude to my mother, and his surprise that the Englishman did not appreciate that she was a 'Fenian'. He was even more surprised when the local Englishmen not only did not put out the Union Jack on the Twelfth of July, Orange Day (high point of the five-month annual season of celebration of Protestantism), but regarded it as a rather strange and un-British thing to do!

Gradually, local Orangemen ceased the practice, and took themselves off to the Twelfth parades with their sashes and bowlers well wrapped up. I must add that the neighbours on either side of us were also from the Shankill area, and better neighbours could hardly have been imagined. The offending neighbour also changed to the point where he offered me a lift on his motorcycle ... 99

> **SOURCE 2** Extract from *Reflections on a Quiet Rebel* by Cal McCrystal, published in 1997. The author, a Catholic journalist, grew up in Belfast in the 1950s in an area which bordered Tiger Bay, at that time a very poor and almost entirely Protestant area of Belfast

66 *One of the poorest of Tiger Bay's families was in fact Catholic. The children walked daily to attend Holy Family Catholic School in Newington. They went to Mass on Sundays. But they were never attacked in Tiger Bay for being Catholics, and never, as far as I know, intimidated into leaving it. Indeed one of the highlights of our year was to join the Tiger Bay revellers on bonfire night and throw scraps of timber onto the roaring flames consuming our Pope.* 99

'Good neighbours'?

Of course, it is dangerous to generalise too much, but all accounts agree that compared to the 1920s and 1930s the 1950s and 1960s were a more peaceful and harmonious time for Northern Ireland.

The key reason was that Northern Ireland was richer and its people more prosperous. However, there were other reasons as well. Let's look at the main factors.

Factor 1: Co-operation during the Second World War

War is often a factor for change in history: sometimes for the better, sometimes for the worse. In this case, the Second World War brought a small but noticeable improvement in relations between the communities in Northern Ireland.

Eire was technically neutral during the Second World War but it was an unusual sort of neutrality. Throughout the war, Allied pilots who parachuted from their aircraft and landed in Eire were returned to their units via Northern Ireland. Another example of de Valera's co-operation with the Allies was the Donegal 'air corridor'. This was an area of Donegal (one of the 26 counties of Eire) which de Valera allowed the Allies to fly over when sending air patrols to hunt down German submarines in the Atlantic. Technically this was neutral air space and the Allies were not supposed to fly over it. However, de Valera allowed the flights because the alternative was a very long detour around the northern end of Donegal. Perhaps the best-known example of co-operation between Eire and the Allies came in 1941 when

1. Look at Sources 1 and 2. What would you say are the strengths and weaknesses of these sources for the historian investigating levels of sectarian tension in the 1950s and early 1960s?

Belfast was bombed, affecting Catholics and Protestants alike. The city was devastated by the bombing and the fires which resulted from the attack. De Valera instantly agreed to requests from Belfast to send fire engines and fire fighters. One journalist working at the time said that this action did more to promote goodwill between the people of Northern Ireland and Eire than the actions of all the politicians since before the time of Gladstone in the 1880s.

SOURCE 3 Eamon de Valera, speaking on 20 April, 1941

66 *I know you will wish me to express on your behalf, on behalf of the Government, our sympathy with the people who are suffering ... In the past, and probably in the present, too, a number of them did not see eye to eye with us politically, but they are our people – we are one and the same people – and their sorrows in the present instance are also our sorrows; and I want to say to them that any help we can give to them in the present time we will give to them whole-heartedly, believing that were the circumstances reversed they would also give us their help whole-heartedly ...* 99

Factor 2: Wartime prosperity

War also reduced unemployment and brought greater prosperity to Northern Ireland. There were huge government orders for food, ships, aeroplanes, clothing and equipment.

Factor 3: The Welfare State

In 1945, many people saw the end of the war as a chance to make a new start and build a better United Kingdom. In the UK general election of 1945, the people voted in a Labour government. This new government proposed a massive 'Welfare State' programme to improve education and tackle the problems of poverty, housing, health and unemployment which had plagued Britain and Northern Ireland in the 1930s. Unionist MPs were happy to accept Labour's plans once it became clear that the British government would pay for them.

The impact of the Welfare State on Northern Ireland was enormous.

- A special Housing Trust built 100,000 desperately needed new houses, which in general were allocated fairly between the communities.
- By 1952, over half a million workers had insurance against illness or unemployment.

- Family Allowance benefited 220,000 children.
- The new National Health Service helped, along with the other reforms, to reduce Northern Ireland's death rate from the highest in the UK in 1939 to the lowest in 1962.
- There was also funding for industrial development. Over 4700 new jobs were created in 1946, and 111 new factories had opened in Northern Ireland by the early 1960s.

All of Northern Ireland's citizens, Protestant and Catholic, shared in this rising prosperity.

SOURCE 4 Extract from *John Hume, Peacemaker*, a biography of the SDLP leader John Hume, published in 1995. The nationalist parade mentioned was in 1947

66 *When [John was] aged only ten, [he] and his father happened to find themselves caught up in a nationalist meeting in a street. There were plenty of waving flags and speakers claiming Irish unity would be the solution to all their problems. Along with everybody else John was getting emotional. Suddenly his father, who was unemployed, put his hand on John's shoulder and said: 'Don't get caught into that, son.' 'Why not, Da?' asked John. 'Because,' his father told him, 'you cannot eat a flag.' John would often repeat that story to people he met. He told me: 'In those early days, politics was about flag-waving, and my view was that politics was about more than that ... politics should be about the everyday problems of the people: housing, jobs.'* 99

2. Make a list of the main benefits brought about by the Welfare State to people in Northern Ireland.
3. Look at Source 4. What did John Hume's father mean when he said, 'You cannot eat a flag'?
4. Explain how this incident affected Hume's attitude to politics.

Factor 4: Education reforms

In 1947, Samuel Hall-Thompson, the Northern Ireland Education Minister, pushed through important reforms in secondary education. He introduced measures such as school meals and scholarships to schools which catered for able pupils. Bright children from poor backgrounds, Catholic or Protestant, now had the chance of a first-class education although schools were still segregated.

Factor 5: Conditions in the Republic of Ireland

Poverty

The prosperity in Northern Ireland contrasted sharply with conditions in the South, by 1949 known as the Irish Republic. Unemployment and poverty were major problems in the Republic throughout the 1950s. Farmers were struggling against foreign competition. There was little industry. The social services in the Republic were no match for those in Northern Ireland. The Republic's young people were forced to emigrate to find a decent standard of living.

ILL-PAID EIRE WORKER: "WOULDN'T I JUST LIKE TO LIVE IN THAT SAME 'BLACK' NORTH!"

SOURCE 6 A cartoon from the journal *The Voice of Ulster*, January 1948

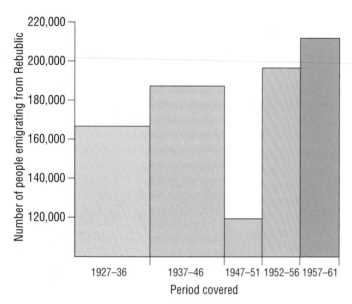

SOURCE 5 Emigration from the Republic, 1926–61

The IRA response

The improvements in Northern Ireland were so significant that the IRA was forced to abandon its military campaign against targets in Northern Ireland. From 1956 to 1962 it had targeted RUC stations, RUC officers and other official Northern Ireland buildings, such as customs posts. Twelve IRA men and six RUC officers were killed in this period.

However, the IRA now had little support among Nationalists (see Source 7). The IRA's aim of a united Ireland seemed irrelevant. Even those Nationalists who did still support the idea were not prepared to use violence to achieve it.

Source 7 gives the IRA's own explanation for why the campaign had failed.

The Catholic Church

The influence of the Catholic Church in the Republic did not always seem to be a force for good, either. The Church blocked attempts to improve hospital care, because this would have meant transferring control of many hospitals from the Church to the state. In 1951, the Republic's pioneering Health Minister Noel Browne tried to introduce a 'Mother and Child Scheme' to give advice and medical care to young mothers. The Church disapproved of this state interference in family life, and the measure was dropped. Browne resigned.

Attitudes to the IRA

The attitude of the Republic's government to the IRA's campaign of violence (see page 56) was also shifting. It co-operated with the Northern Ireland authorities in hunting down the IRA members. By 1958, most of the key IRA activists were in prison.

SOURCE 7 An extract from the secret IRA journal *An tÓglach* (*The Volunteer*)

> 1. The fact that the people see no connection between the fight in the North and the idea of improving the Irish social conditions, etc.
> 2. A lack of resources ... money and the right type of weapons.
> 3. The lack of an efficient publicity and propaganda machine.
> 4. A dwindling of public support both North and South, making it virtually impossible for men to operate on guerrilla lines – one of the basic ingredients for a successful guerrilla campaign is the support of wide sections of the people. This comes only from an awareness and understanding of the reasons for and nature of the struggle.

Optimism

There was no doubting the sense of optimism in Northern Ireland in the 1960s. The ECUMENICAL movement was promoting co-operation and understanding between the Catholic Church and other Christian faiths. In 1963, Captain Terence O'Neill became the new leader of the Unionist Party and the Northern Ireland Prime Minister. He tried to build a relationship of friendship and trust with Northern Ireland's Catholics and with the Republic. He visited Catholic schools and made other friendly gestures to Northern Ireland's Catholics. He invited the TAOISEACH (pronounced Tee-shock), Sean Lemass, to visit him in Belfast in January 1965.

O'Neill was convinced that most people in Northern Ireland, Protestant or Catholic, were not full of sectarian fear and hate. He believed that they wanted Northern Ireland to become like any other forward-looking modern state, more interested in creating jobs and developing industry, and in modernisation and democracy than in forever looking back on old arguments. The Northern Ireland elections of November 1965 seemed to prove O'Neill right. Electors gave his policies massive support, as the Unionists gained their highest ever share of the Northern Ireland vote (well over 60 per cent).

In 1967 a new Taoiseach, Jack Lynch, was elected in the Republic. O'Neill met him as well, and made a point of shaking his hand publicly, in front of the cameras of the press. To the watching world, the prospect of peace for Northern Ireland must have appeared greater than ever. Others did not see it in that way, as you will soon find out.

■ ACTIVITY A

You are writing a short item for a radio broadcast in 1962. You have got hold of a leaked copy of Source 7. The aim is to report the news of the end of the IRA campaign and the reasons why it has failed. You have a limit for your item of 350 words. Your item should cover

■ the end of the IRA campaign
■ how economic prosperity has reduced sectarian tension
■ why many Northern Ireland Nationalists may not wish to be part of the Irish Republic
■ any other factors.

You could add a conclusion explaining what you think the most important factors or combinations of factors were.

SOURCE 8 O'Neill describes his work to gain the confidence of Catholics in his autobiography, 1972

66 I spent a lot of time during the election canvassing Catholic and Protestant houses in Belfast . . . In both I had a tremendous reception. No previous Prime Minister of Northern Ireland had canvassed in Catholic houses for Unionist votes, but my reception in Protestant houses was equally warm . . . We swept the country to a degree which surprised even myself. Co-operation between North and South was now publicly endorsed. 99

■ ACTIVITY B

You are Terence O'Neill. It is the mid-1960s, and you are about to make a sales pitch to a group of American business executives, explaining to them why now is a great time to invest in Northern Ireland. Write down what you plan to say, and what points you will make to show that Northern Ireland is the new land of optimism and opportunity.

SOURCE 9 O'Neill and Taoiseach Sean Lemass at Stormont in 1965

'**W**hy is a young man like you concerned about Northern Ireland?'

IN 1967, A YOUNG British Labour MP called Paul Rose asked for a meeting with Barbara Castle. She was the Minister responsible for Northern Ireland. He had just returned from a visit to Northern Ireland and was deeply concerned that conflict could erupt at any time. Source 1 gives Barbara Castle's reaction.

> **S**OURCE 1 Barbara Castle's response to Paul Rose, 1967. At this time there was a major war in Vietnam and Rhodesia was struggling to gain independence from Britain
>
> 66 *I remember Barbara Castle patting me on the head and saying, 'Why is a young man like you concerned about Northern Ireland? What about Vietnam? What about Rhodesia?' I just looked at her with incomprehension and said, 'You'll see when they start shooting one another.' She was totally oblivious to this. I think the British government's priorities were focused on other things to the extent that they were totally blinded to what was going on in their own backyard.* 99

■ ACTIVITY

Why was Paul Rose so concerned about Northern Ireland? You are going to help him prepare his reply.

The headings in this table will guide you through the next six pages. Fill out your own copy of the table as you go along.

Issue	Example	A new problem or an old one?	Why it matters
Divisions in society • education • religion • daily life			
Economic problems			
Divisions amongst Unionists • extremist groups • opposition to O'Neill • discontented working-class Unionists			
Civil rights • local government • other areas (law, education, housing, employment)			

Ignorance

For Nationalists and Unionists really to understand each other, they needed to meet. This was not common.

Segregated education

The Churches had blocked all attempts to create a non-religious state education system in the 1920s and again in the 1940s. Despite improvements in education, the school system was still largely segregated in the 1960s. There were mixed colleges or universities where educated people met people from other communities. However, this involved only a small minority, most of whom were middle class. Most Catholic and Protestant youngsters played different sports, and went to different scout troops, youth clubs or other organisations.

Segregated employment

Many industries or businesses employed only Catholics or only Protestants. This was not usually a deliberate policy. Often it was connected to the location of the business. For example, the workforce in the Bushmills whiskey distillery in County Antrim was mainly Protestant because it was situated in a Protestant area. In the 1950s and 1960s, many people were given jobs on the basis of a recommendation from family or friends rather than through a formal application and interview. Thus a foreman on a building site might employ someone from his own community because he knew that person to be reliable. He probably knew very few people from the other community well enough to make a judgement about them.

> **S**OURCE 2 An extract from *Reflections on a Quiet Rebel* by Cal McCrystal. The author is a Catholic who grew up in Northern Ireland. He is now a journalist for the *Observer* newspaper
>
> 66 *... prejudices were widespread among Catholics, rural and urban. They were narrowly dogmatic [stuck to their beliefs] and unyieldingly bigoted [prejudiced]. The Church was one source of this. Priests at Mass spoke from the pulpit about non-Catholics – rather than about Presbyterians, Methodists, Church of Ireland members – as though to underline an assertion that if you were not a Catholic you were nothing at all.*
> *... Catholics swallowed whole the Church's insistence on censoring 'evil' books detrimental to traditional Catholic Irish values ... And they thoroughly approved of the Irish Cardinal MacRory's claim in 1931 that the Church of Ireland was not even part of the Church of Christ.* 99

SOURCE 3 Extract from *No Surrender*, by R. Harbinson. In this book the author, a Protestant, describes growing up in a Protestant area, and how his schooling left large gaps in his knowledge

66 *Our schools drummed into us over and over again the Protestant story ... The particular rack on which they tortured us appeared in the form of a small, buff-coloured booklet entitled* How we differ from Rome ... *Our ignorance of the Catholic world was profound. I, for instance, believed that Mickeys [Catholics] existed only in parts of Belfast and nowhere else except the Free State and Rome itself. That many Catholics were living in London, or were allowed to live in London with our Protestant king, seemed impossible.* 99

The result: prejudice

Since Nationalists and Unionists usually lived, went to school and worked separately, the communities knew very little about each other. All too often the gaps in their knowledge were filled by prejudice. Sources 2 and 3 give two extreme examples of this.

1. Imagine you are one of the teachers in the school described in Source 3. What would your reaction be to Source 2?
2. Imagine you are one of the Catholics described in Source 2. How would you react to Source 3?

■ TASK A

Fill in the 'Divisions in society' section of your table.

Economic problems

The improved relations of the 1950s and 1960s were built on economic prosperity. But this turned out to be a shaky foundation.

Northern Ireland's economy had major weaknesses. Its industries, particularly shipbuilding and textiles, were old and expensive to run. They could not compete with the new industries developing in Scandinavia and the Far East. In the early 1960s, Belfast's largest employer, Harland and Wolff, began to close down its shipyards. By 1965 only one remained. The year 1966 saw the closure of Belfast's rope works, the largest in the world. All of these closures meant job losses. In Northern Ireland, unemployment was between six and seven per cent, over three times the UK national average. But some areas, such as West Belfast, had unemployment in the region of eighteen per cent, which hit both Protestants and Catholics alike.

Despite the achievements of the Welfare State, Northern Ireland still had some of the worst slum housing in Europe (see Source 4). Protests over housing in the late 1960s focused on conditions for Catholic families. However, very large numbers of Protestant families also lived in terrible conditions.

In the past, economic problems had spilled over into sectarian tension. This could happen again.

■ TASK B

Fill in the 'Economic problems' section of your table.

SOURCE 4 Slum housing conditions in mainly Protestant Belfast (left) and mainly Catholic Londonderry. In towns and cities in Northern Ireland in the 1960s both Catholics and Protestants had to live in terrible conditions

Divisions among Unionists

Ian Paisley

O'Neill's friendly gestures towards the Catholics and the Republic earned him many supporters. However, he also made some powerful and extremist enemies. Ian Paisley made his name protesting about O'Neill's concessions to Catholics and against the involvement of Northern Ireland churches in the ecumenical movement. He and his followers pursued O'Neill at every opportunity, demanding his resignation. Paisley, who had formed his own Free Presbyterian Church in 1951, at the age of 25, set up the Ulster Protestant Action group and used his own newspaper, the *Protestant Telegraph*, to get his message across. Paisley claimed that the Catholic Church was a threat to Ulster's Protestant heritage, and so O'Neill's gestures of friendship to the Catholics in Northern Ireland and the Republic were a threat as well.

Paisley built up a strong base of incredibly dedicated and loyal supporters. His demonstrations often ended in violence, such as when he demanded the removal of the Irish flag from a window in the Catholic Divis Street area of Belfast in 1964. Even so, he seemed to be touching on a deep concern that many hardline Unionists, or Loyalists, felt about O'Neill's actions.

Most politicians in Britain and Northern Ireland at the time underestimated Paisley and were puzzled by him. His views seemed to belong more to the seventeenth century than the twentieth, and he was seen as a religious fanatic. However, he was also a clever politician, an inspirational leader and an extremely good organiser.

Ian Paisley, now the leader of the Democratic Unionist Party, remains a controversial and confusing figure today. His views inevitably feed sectarian hatred. Some experts on the IRA have suggested that he has not been murdered by the IRA because his extremist views persuade so many new members to join it.

3. Why was Paisley underestimated? What evidence suggests that this was a bad error?

SOURCE 5 Ian Paisley speaking at an election rally in the late 1960s

Opposition to O'Neill

Some members of O'Neill's own Unionist Party found him rather cold and quite difficult to work with. His background was in the landed aristocracy, and he could come across as something of a snob. His critics disliked his way of acting without consulting his colleagues, such as when he invited Taoiseach Sean Lemass to Belfast in 1965. O'Neill was more widely liked and respected outside Northern Ireland than within it. His colleagues were irritated by the way the media showed O'Neill as the only Unionist with any vision. Some of his colleagues within the Unionist Party began to plot against him.

Discontent among working-class Unionists

The living and working conditions of many Protestant working-class people were dreadful. Northern Ireland had some of the worst housing problems in Europe, affecting both Catholics and Protestants. Rising unemployment hit Protestant families as well as Catholic families. Some Protestants asked themselves what being a Protestant in a Protestant state had really given them.

The UVF

The IRA may have abandoned its campaign, but republican ideas had not gone away. In 1966, the Irish Republic celebrated the 50th anniversary of the Easter Rising (see pages 44–45). Some politicians in the Republic made speeches criticising Northern Ireland and calling for an end to Partition. Republicans in the North also celebrated the Easter Rising and many Protestants were alarmed by the large processions celebrating this event. It seemed to confirm fears that Northern Ireland Nationalists were the enemy within.

Protestants feared a renewed IRA campaign of violence, and in May 1966 some extreme Unionists formed a new paramilitary group. It was called the Ulster Volunteer Force, after the original UVF created in 1913, although it was nothing like the mass movement that the original UVF had been. Soon after its formation, the new UVF murdered a young Catholic. O'Neill used the Special Powers Act to ban the organisation, but it was not so easy to get rid of the fears and prejudices that lay behind it. The Special Powers Act was introduced when the state of Northern Ireland was formed in April 1922 as a measure to counter the IRA threat to Northern Ireland. It allowed for imprisonment without trial, and even sentencing to death in extreme cases. It was seen by Nationalists as a symbol of oppression and by Loyalists as a necessary bastion of defence. Thus, O'Neill's use of the Act against Loyalists was a shock to many.

SOURCE 6 William Smith, son of a shipyard worker in Belfast, who later became chairman of the Progressive Unionist Party, speaking in the 1990s

66 *There was an elite grouping within the Unionist Party who were the aristocracy, the landowners, the rich, and they manipulated the situation in Stormont [the Northern Ireland Parliament] for 70 years. So when people talk about misrule in Stormont I would agree with them. But I would say it was misrule of Catholics **and** Protestants, not just Catholics.* 99

■ TASK

Fill in the 'Divisions among Unionists' section of your table.

Growing concerns about civil rights

Another concern for O'Neill's government was the fact that despite the improvements of the 1950s and 1960s there was still glaring inequality and discrimination in Northern Ireland.

Employment

- Most of the new industries and investment which O'Neill brought to Northern Ireland ended up in the unionist strongholds of the north and east of the Province. Of the 111 new factories built in Northern Ireland in the post-war period to the mid-1960s, only sixteen were built in Counties Londonderry, Tyrone and Fermanagh – counties with nationalist majorities or populations which were finely balanced between the nationalist and unionist communities. This upset Unionists in those counties as well as Nationalists.
- The giant Harland and Wolff shipyard did not seem to have changed its employment policies since the late nineteenth century. It employed 10,000 workers, of whom only 400 were Catholics.
- Few Catholics were employed in the civil service, and promotion for them was rare.
- In Londonderry, an area with a Catholic majority, the highest-ranking Catholic in the education department was the official in charge of school meals.

The law

The RUC was overwhelmingly Protestant, with about six times as many Protestant officers as Catholics. Another Catholic complaint was that so many RUC police officers seemed to be members of the Orange Order. Since one of the fundamental rules of the Order was to oppose Catholicism, Catholics felt that belonging to it was not appropriate for employees of a public service. The B-Specials were even more controversial. There were around 10,000 B-Specials, part-time, armed volunteer constables who could be called up for emergency service. They were almost all Protestant, and had a very bad reputation for harassing Catholics and using violence indiscriminately. However, supporters and defenders of the RUC and the B-Specials claim that republican activists discouraged Catholics from joining the force (using force and intimidation if they had to).

Politics

- Politics in Northern Ireland was dominated by the Ulster Unionist Party. By the 1960s many people, especially young Nationalists, were disillusioned with the way politics worked in the Province. Many blamed the Unionist party, but some pointed out that Nationalists had not played a constructive role in Northern Ireland's politics either (see Source 7).
- In the city of Londonderry, there was blatant vote rigging, or gerrymandering (see Source 8). While 14,000 Catholics were represented by eight nationalist councillors, 9000 Protestant voters ended up with twelve councillors.
- Voting in local elections in Northern Ireland was on the basis of property. Only ratepayers voted, so if you did not own property you could not vote, and if you owned several properties you could have more than one vote. This discriminated against the generally poorer Catholic population.

Housing

- The Housing Trust had allocated new dwellings fairly (see page 59), but local councils did not. Two thirds of the houses built by local authorities after the war went to Protestants (householders were entitled to vote in the local elections, so the authorities tried to cut down the number of Catholic householders). Nationalist councils were also guilty. In Newry (mainly nationalist), the local authority built 765 council houses, of which only 22 went to Protestants.

Education

In 1965, the government announced that Northern Ireland's second university would be built in Coleraine, a small, mainly Protestant, town in Antrim, rather than in Londonderry, which was clearly the second city of the province. Ordinary Protestants and Catholics alike were outraged, especially as it appeared that Londonderry's Unionists had blocked the plans for the university to be in their city because this would attract still more Catholics to live there. Protestants joined Catholics in a 'University for Derry' campaign.

SOURCE 7 Extract from an article written by John Hume in the *Irish Times* newspaper, 1964

66 *Weak opposition leads to corrupt government. Nationalists in opposition have been in no way constructive. They have – quite rightly – been loud in their demands for rights, but they have remained silent and inactive about their duties. In 40 years of opposition they have not produced one constructive contribution on either the social or economic plane to the development of Northern Ireland ... leadership has been the comfortable leadership of flags and slogans. Easy, no doubt, but irresponsible ... It is this lack of positive contribution and the apparent lack of interest in the general welfare of Northern Ireland that has led many Protestants to believe that the Northern Catholic is politically irresponsible and therefore unfit to rule.* 99

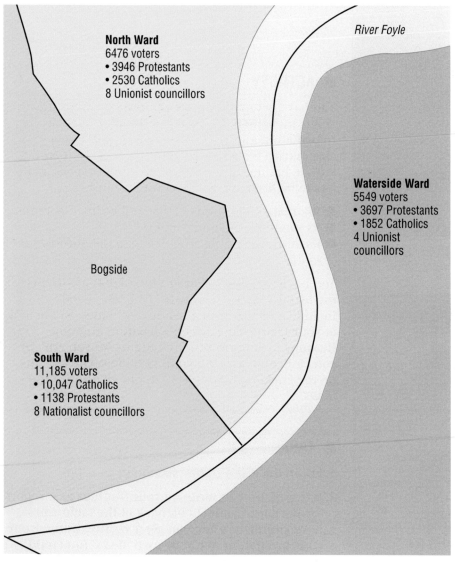

River Foyle

North Ward
6476 voters
• 3946 Protestants
• 2530 Catholics
8 Unionist councillors

Waterside Ward
5549 voters
• 3697 Protestants
• 1852 Catholics
4 Unionist councillors

Bogside

South Ward
11,185 voters
• 10,047 Catholics
• 1138 Protestants
8 Nationalist councillors

SOURCE 8 Local government in Londonderry

The NICRA

By the late 1960s, there was a generation of well-educated and ambitious middle-class Catholics in Northern Ireland. They were fully aware of their rights, were frustrated by the STATUS QUO, and wanted to expose discrimination. They did not want to end Partition or to overthrow the Northern Ireland state. Instead, they wanted to play a full role in it, in particular in government or the professions. They wanted to sweep away the prejudices and discrimination that stood in their way.

They compared themselves to the successful black civil rights movement in the southern states of the USA. Through protests and demonstrations, the black civil rights activists had forced the US Congress to pass Civil Rights Acts in 1964 and 1965.

The Northern Ireland Civil Rights Association (NICRA) was formed in February 1967. A wide range of organisations and individuals, including trade unions and members of political parties, signed up to the new organisation, not just discontented Catholics. Catholic and Protestant students from Northern Ireland's universities and colleges were heavily involved, including both socialists and conservatives. The NICRA stated its aims as follows:

■ To defend the basic freedoms of all citizens.
■ To protect the rights of the individual.
■ To highlight all possible abuses of power.
■ To demand guarantees for freedom of speech, assembly and association (belonging to a trade union).
■ To inform the public of their lawful rights.

67

The NICRA immediately raised awareness of discrimination. Many middle-class Protestants (who were usually Unionists) had not previously been aware of discrimination, and were dismayed about it when they did find out. An opinion poll in December 1967 showed that 43 per cent of the population favoured new laws outlawing discrimination.

SOURCE 9 B-Specials searching a civilian during the IRA campaigns against Northern Ireland in the early 1960s

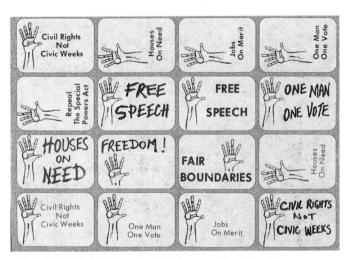

SOURCE 10 Sheets of stickers produced by the NICRA. These stickers were meant to be handed out to passers-by in town centres to raise awareness of the aims of the movement

The year 1968 saw student demonstrations against governments and their policies in many parts of the world. In France, student protests about government policies resulted in serious violence. In the USA, students demonstrated against their country's involvement in a war in Vietnam. In Czechoslovakia, students led campaigns for greater freedom of speech in their own country.

Student members of the NICRA attempted to hold their own protests. However, the Northern Ireland government blocked any attempts by the NICRA to hold meetings or demonstrations. By the summer of 1968, frustration was setting in. Unknown to the NICRA members, however, the civil rights movement was on the verge of a historic development, which is the subject of Chapter 5.

■ ACTIVITY

You have been asked to produce a leaflet for the civil rights movement in Northern Ireland. Use the information and sources on pages 66–68 to summarise the aims of the movement. Your leaflet will be handed out to people in town centres, so it has to be brief and to the point. It should cover

- the main complaints of the civil rights movement
- its membership and support
- its aims, including what it wants the government to do.

You have to keep to a strict limit of 200 words so that the leaflet is not too crowded. You also need to include a picture and a heading to make people look at your leaflet. One possible heading might be: 'Five Reasons to Support the Civil Rights Movement'; or you can come up with your own idea. The slogans on the stickers in Source 10 might give you some ideas.

■ TASK

1. Fill in the 'Civil rights' section of your table.

2. It is now time to write up your findings as a report for Barbara Castle. Look back at the table you have completed. You can get a writing frame from your teacher, or use your own ideas. You could write a full report or make notes to help you with an oral presentation.

chapter 5

WHY DID CONFLICT BREAK OUT IN NORTHERN IRELAND IN 1968–71?

> 66 *We never thought of the IRA being regenerated. As far as we were concerned we were a new generation with a completely new approach, totally based on non-violence.* 99

Fast track: Were the Troubles inevitable?

COMPARE SOURCES 1 and 2. They highlight the change in Northern Ireland from peaceful protest in mid-1968 to bitter street fighting and an armed IRA campaign by 1971.

The slide into violence began with the civil rights campaigns of 1968, but that was never their intention. In the previous chapter, you have seen that some people were predicting bloodshed in Northern Ireland, but they were a small minority. If the civil rights marchers who set out in October 1968 had known that they were about to trigger off 30 years of disastrous conflict, they would almost certainly not have carried on. However, they did, and violence followed. In this chapter, you will examine how and why this happened. There are three key issues to explore:

- How did the civil rights marches of 1968 trigger violence in 1968 and 1969?
- Why were British troops sent to Northern Ireland in 1969?
- What were the causes and consequences of the re-emergence of the IRA?

SOURCE 1 Nationalist MP and civil rights campaigner Austin Currie who organised a sit-in protest in Caledon, near Dungannon in County Tyrone, June 1968. Currie was trying to highlight discrimination by the local council in the allocation of council housing to local people – the house had been allocated to a single Protestant woman rather than a Catholic family with children

■ ACTIVITY

Overview: Northern Ireland 1968–71

Work in pairs. Read through the following events of 1968–71. Try to agree on the following:

- why civil rights protests led to violence
- the point when you think the conflict we generally call the 'Troubles' began (there is a lot of debate as to the precise point at which the conflict started).

At this point you are only using an outline of the events which are described in more detail later in the chapter. When you have finished the chapter you can see whether your views have changed.

June–October 1968: Row as RUC breaks up civil rights march

Tension began to rise in Northern Ireland when a Nationalist MP, Austin Currie, organised a sit-in protest in a house in County Tyrone (see Source 1). A series of marches followed this protest, aiming to highlight the issue of discrimination in Northern Ireland. In October 1968, RUC officers broke up a march to the centre of Londonderry. The media reported the event widely. The Nationalist Party at Stormont withdrew its MPs in protest at the treatment of the marchers.

November–December 1968: Unionist anger at civil rights movement

Further civil rights marches followed. The British government in London pressed the Northern Ireland Prime Minister Terence O'Neill to pass anti-discrimination measures in Northern Ireland.

The reforms were passed, but the tension continued to rise. Some Unionists were concerned that the pace of O'Neill's reforms was too fast. Others feared that the civil rights movement was an attempt by Republicans to destroy the Northern Ireland state. Many working-class Protestants resented the impression given in the media that only Catholics suffered poverty and hardship. O'Neill called for calm, describing Ulster as being at a crossroads, needing to choose between becoming a modern democratic state or remaining a backward place of ignorance and prejudice.

SOURCE 2 British troops stand well back as a petrol bomb explodes in the Falls Road area of Belfast in March 1971

January–April 1969: O'Neill forced to resign

In January 1969, militants within the civil rights movement decided to keep the pressure on O'Neill by holding a march from Belfast to Londonderry. A mob of militant Loyalists ambushed the marchers, but the police did little to protect them. Serious rioting followed in Londonderry. O'Neill called an election to make the most of the support he had among the Protestant and Catholic middle classes. He won, but not convincingly. The hardliners were now dictating the pace in Northern Ireland. April saw more civil rights marches and more violence, especially in Belfast. O'Neill resigned and was replaced by James Chichester-Clark.

Summer 1969: British troops on the streets of Northern Ireland

Tension increased further as the summer marching season approached. The Londonderry Apprentice Boys' march was followed by large-scale riots between police and residents of the Catholic Bogside district, in what became known as the Battle of the Bogside. The violence spread to Belfast. Thousands of people were burned out of their homes, and there seemed to be a real possibility of a massacre of the city's Catholics. In August, the British government agreed to send in troops to keep the warring factions apart.

Autumn 1969–70: Revival of the IRA

Troops soon clashed with both Protestant and Catholic crowds, and were often accused of using excessive violence. They killed two Protestants in a protest on the Shankill Road in October 1969. Behind the scenes, the IRA was re-forming. The newly formed Provisional IRA and the old Official IRA both recruited activists and gathered weapons. The Provisionals were more active, defending Catholic areas against attacks from loyalist militants. Unionists were appalled, and Prime Minister Chichester-Clark ordered the army to search the Falls Road for weapons and IRA suspects. This was a key event, in that it turned many Nationalists against the army, and increased support for the IRA. The IRA exploited the situation, destroying Protestant-owned businesses and attacking troops and RUC officers.

How did the civil rights marches of 1968 lead to violence?

The aims of the civil rights movement

The aims of the civil rights movement were simple. Its members wanted all citizens of Northern Ireland to have equal civil rights. They wanted to end sectarian discrimination in employment, housing, law and other areas. It was not a solely republican movement, but attracted wide support.

- Catholics/Republicans supported it because Catholics generally suffered the worst discrimination, but most Protestants/Unionists also supported the civil rights movement's demand for an end to discrimination.
- Many socialists also supported the movement, since their main aim was to build a society where wealth was shared out equally among all people.

■ TASK

1. Write some newspaper headlines about Austin Currie's sit-in (see below) as they might appear in:

- a local unionist paper
- a local nationalist paper
- a British daily newspaper
- an American newspaper.

You could produce radio soundbites rather than headlines.

2. Explain why your headlines are different, and how you made them different.

Three steps to violent conflict

Step 1: Austin Currie's sit-in

In June 1968, a nineteen-year-old woman, Miss Emily Beattie, was allocated a council house in the small village of Caledon (near Dungannon in County Tyrone). Before she could move in, Austin Currie, the Nationalist MP for East Tyrone, decided to protest. He staged a sit-in in her house. The police soon removed him, but television cameras were there, and local news programmes covered the event. Currie was able to point out to the public that this case was an example of the sectarian bias in the way houses were allocated. As a single young woman, Miss Beattie hardly qualified ahead of couples with children on the priority housing list. It was said she had been 'preferred' because she was secretary to a member of the Ulster Unionist Party. The point was also made that the policeman who removed Currie from the house was Miss Beattie's brother!

Step 2: A peaceful march to Dungannon

Currie contacted the Northern Ireland Civil Rights Association (NICRA), which was interested in taking up this issue. Currie suggested a high-profile march from Coalisland to Dungannon, which would highlight discrimination against Catholics. For example, the NICRA argued that although Catholics had about 53 per cent of the vote in local elections in Dungannon, boundary fixing meant that there were fourteen unionist councillors to seven nationalist.

The march went ahead on 24 August. Some 2500 marchers walked from Coalisland to the edge of Dungannon carrying placards saying things like 'One Man, One House, One Job' and 'Jobs on Merit'. The marchers had intended to march into Dungannon and stage a public rally, but 400 police stopped them. There was no trouble.

Step 3: Violence in Londonderry

Two members of the Londonderry Housing Action Committee were on the Dungannon march. They suggested that a civil rights rally should be held in their city. The date was fixed for 5 October 1968, and the media were told about it.

However, the Londonderry march was banned from entering the city centre by William Craig, Northern Ireland's Home Affairs Minister. Under the Special Powers Act Craig could ban any march without giving a reason. Perhaps he feared civil disorder, or he shared the view of many that this was just a republican march. The ban focused attention on the march and made the demonstrators more determined. They ignored the ban and tried to get to the Diamond, the main square in the centre of the city, via the Craigavon Bridge. But at the bridge they were met by RUC constables and barricades. Following his orders from the government, the RUC commander refused to let them cross the bridge. Television cameras were on hand to record what happened next.

Within a short time, the bridge was a scene of violent confusion as marchers tried to cross and RUC men tried to prevent them. The television news in Northern Ireland that night showed police armoured cars using water cannon to disperse the crowd, but not much else. However, RTE, the Republic's broadcasting company, showed much more. Viewers in the Republic saw dramatic pictures of RUC officers beating retreating civilians mercilessly with batons and innocent bystanders being flattened by water cannon. The impression given was that Northern Ireland was an oppressive, intolerant state.

SOURCE 1 A demonstrator being struck by RUC officers at the civil rights rally of 5 October 1968

November 1968

Government concessions

The Londonderry violence triggered more civil rights demonstrations and more violence. The usual pattern was that civil rights marches stirred up loyalist outrage because loyalists saw the marchers not as civil rights campaigners but as Republicans. These confrontations usually led to police intervention, generally even-handed but sometimes with the sectarian excesses seen in Londonderry. Some historians believe that some marches were organised specifically to stretch the RUC.

In October and November the Province saw more civil rights demonstrations and more violence. These months also saw furious political activity between the government in Northern Ireland and the British Prime Minister Harold Wilson. Wilson's government has to take much of the blame for the outbreak of violence in Northern Ireland. From the time he came to power in 1964 he completely ignored the situation in Northern Ireland, even though he was warned about the rising tension. As the tension rose Wilson put pressure on O'Neill to act decisively and do something quickly to reduce discrimination. On 22 November 1968, O'Neill announced a package of reforms. They may not seem radical today, but they were the biggest concessions by the Unionist-dominated Stormont government in 50 years. The reforms were:

- The Londonderry Corporation (the local government of Londonderry, which had been elected on the gerrymandered system giving Unionists a majority) was suspended and replaced by an appointed commission which took over all of its functions. The appointed commission consisted of people who were effectively civil servants who would run services and facilities until democratic reforms took place and a new Corporation was elected.
- Local councils would allocate housing on a needs-related points system, so that those most in need were given houses.
- Some of the powers of the Northern Ireland government's Special Powers Act were to be removed.
- An independent OMBUDSMAN would investigate complaints against local authorities.
- The principle of universal suffrage (one person one vote, regardless of whether or not they owned property) in local elections would be *considered*.

1. Do you regard these reforms as major steps by the Unionist government? Explain your answer.
2. Do you think these reforms would have taken place without pressure from the British government?
3. Does the British government deserve much credit for this? Explain your answer.

December 1968

'Ulster at a crossroads'

The civil rights leaders agreed to suspend their protests to allow the reforms time to have some effect. Despite this breathing space, O'Neill soon found himself in a very difficult position, trying to be a moderate in a country which was becoming increasingly extremist. Ian Paisley accused him of betraying Protestants while militant Catholics were soon criticising him as well.

Even so, the majority of people, Protestant and Catholic, supported O'Neill. The majority of people in Northern Ireland were *not* extremists.

In December, O'Neill made a speech on television. He spoke of Ulster at a crossroads, and appealed for peace and moderation (Source 2).

SOURCE 2 An extract from O'Neill's speech, 9 December 1968

❝ What kind of Ulster do you want? A happy respected province ... or a place continually torn apart by riots and demonstrations, and regarded by the rest of Britain as a political outcast? ❞

1 January 1969

The People's Democracy march

The reforms of 22 November brought five weeks of peace. Then, on New Year's Day 1969, about 40 young people, mainly student supporters of People's Democracy, set out to walk across Northern Ireland from Belfast to Londonderry.

People's Democracy was a fringe movement within the civil rights campaign. Its members were mainly militant socialist students, led by Eamon McCann, Michael Farrell and Bernadette Devlin. Devlin was quite open about their aims. She said they wanted to break the truce between O'Neill and the civil rights movement, and to show people that O'Neill was offering them nothing.

It was a three-day march. On the first two days, the march was re-routed several times by the RUC to avoid confrontation with loyalist counter-marchers and demonstrators who formed human barricades across the civil rights marchers' intended routes. Some of these counter-marchers were led by Paisley himself. The march was closely followed by television cameras.

On the third day, marchers were at Burntollet near the city of Londonderry. There they were suddenly ambushed by a loyalist mob. The television cameras were there, of course. They showed protesters being showered with bricks, bottles and stones. Then the mob closed in and beat the marchers with iron bars

SOURCE 3 An early People's Democracy poster. The glove was the symbol of 'black power' used by civil rights activists in the USA

and sticks. Most alarmingly, the RUC escort, supposedly there to prevent conflict, appeared to do little to protect the marchers. Later investigations showed that some of the mob were actually off-duty police or special constables. That night, the city of Londonderry was swept by further rioting and violence by loyalist mobs. RUC officers and B-Specials invaded the Catholic Bogside area, smashing shops, breaking windows and singing Protestant songs.

SOURCE 4 Crowd violence as loyalists ambush civil rights marchers at Burntollet in January 1969

SOURCE 5 Michael Farrell, the Peace Movement march organiser, being interviewed by RTE on 2 January 1969

66 *We've had a very good turn-out. Now we've had some difficulties along the route and there are certain towns we've been prevented from going through. We don't like that, but we feel that demonstrates the fact that in Northern Ireland we have a situation like the southern states of America, where you do not have the basic democratic liberty of free procession.* 99

4. Would you say that Sources 4 and 5 are more useful together than they are separately? Explain your answer.

SOURCE 6 Dr Raymond Maclean. Dr Maclean served in the RAF before practising as a doctor in Londonderry. He was part of the early civil rights movement

66 *For several hours, I was busy treating injured marchers. I, and the first-aiders helping me, were horrified to hear the stories recounted by the injured as to what had happened when they approached Burntollet Bridge. The most amazing and consistent thread throughout the various stories was the complete lack of intervention or assistance given to any of the marchers by the large body of police present, all of whom witnessed the grievous bodily assault carried out by the loyalist militants against the marchers, who were unarmed themselves and had apparently refused to retaliate.* 99

SOURCE 7 Extracts from the report of the Cameron COMMISSION, the government inquiry into the outbreak of violence in 1968–69

66 *... A number of policemen were guilty of misconduct which involved assault and battery, malicious damage to property ... and the use of provocative sectarian and political slogans ... Not only do we find these allegations of misconduct are substantiated but that for such conduct among members of a disciplined and well-led force there can be no acceptable justification or excuse.* 99

February 1969

The fall of O'Neill

O'Neill tried to continue his moderate policies, but he had lost the support of his own MPs. He decided to ask the people of Northern Ireland to give their opinion of his 'moderate' position. He called an election for 24 February. Ian Paisley stood against him in his own constituency.

The People's Democracy activist Michael Farrell also stood against O'Neill. He had no chance of winning. What he did achieve was to take over 2000 Catholic votes which O'Neill would probably have gained. This meant that O'Neill's winning margin over Paisley in his constituency was much smaller than it would otherwise have been. The election result undermined O'Neill and boosted Paisley. O'Neill won the election overall, but only just.

■ TASK

Consider O'Neill's position in 1969. Would you say he was in an impossible situation? O'Neill's critics saw him as a failure or, even worse, a traitor. Look at the following statements and explain how far you think each one is justified.

'O'Neill betrayed Protestants in Northern Ireland.'

'Some Protestants felt that O'Neill had betrayed them.'

'Catholics and Nationalists appreciated the efforts O'Neill made to improve relations with them.'

'Many Catholics felt that O'Neill's reforms were only skin deep and that he was not sincere.'

'O'Neill was more highly regarded outside Northern Ireland than he was in Northern Ireland.'

You could mark each statement on a scale of 1 to 5, with 1 meaning you totally agree and 5 meaning you totally disagree.

A series of bomb explosions now increased tension still further. More Unionist MPs turned against O'Neill because they thought the IRA was in action again, although it was later discovered that the bombs were in fact planted by Loyalists to incriminate Republicans. By now the militants had the upper hand, and Northern Ireland was getting out of control. O'Neill was finally forced to resign on 28 April 1969.

Why was the reaction to the civil rights movement so violent?

So far we have been simply telling the story. We have not been analysing why the civil rights campaign led to violence. Let's retrace our steps and look at the factors that played a part.

Media attention
The entire saga took place under the gaze of the television cameras. This raised the stakes and heightened confrontation.

Sectarian prejudice
Clearly, long-standing sectarian prejudice played a major part in explaining the long-term civil rights abuses. It was also one reason for the violence in 1969. The government's own report (by the Cameron Commission) went out of its way to criticise the sectarian bias in the actions of some RUC officers and B-Specials. It made it clear that the marchers were not violent.

Fear of the IRA
Many Protestants, including many in the Northern Ireland government, saw the civil rights movement as a plot to destabilise Northern Ireland, little more than a front for an IRA attack backed up by the Republic.
  With hindsight, this may seem to be nonsense. The IRA was virtually non-existent at this time. However, what people *think* is true is more important than what *is* true. Many of the Protestant population in Northern Ireland did not question whether this threat was real. They had seen thousands of Catholics turn out to parades commemorating the 50th anniversary of the Easter Rising in 1966.
  This strengthened their fears that Catholics in Northern Ireland were a secret republican army. Some politicians in the Republic made tensions worse. Charles Haughey (later to become Taoiseach) was suspended from the government under suspicion of helping to fund the IRA (see page 82).

Working-class Protestant resentment
Many working-class Loyalists were angry at the demands of the 'civil righters'. They resented the impression given in the media that only Catholics suffered hardships while a privileged Protestant community looked down on them. They also had to deal with poor living conditions and hardship.

Why was the reaction to the civil rights movement so violent?

Radicalism in the civil rights movement
The NICRA was concerned first and foremost with the issue of civil rights, and many Protestants supported this. However, some of the leading figures in the civil rights movement were republican Nationalists. Many others believed in socialist principles, especially the leaders of the People's Democracy movement. Northern Ireland was a very conservative society, and socialist ideas were still treated with suspicion.

O'Neill's failings
O'Neill was a moderate politician, who found it very difficult to deal with extremists. His reforms were hurried. They were too radical for his unionist critics, but not radical enough for his republican critics.

Marching and confrontation
Marching has a long tradition in Northern Ireland. It has often led to confrontation. The People's Democracy march in January 1969 deliberately took a route through sensitive areas, which would be sure to stir up Protestant hostility.

SOURCE 8 From Bernadette Devlin's first speech in the House of Commons in late 1969. She became an MP in Westminster after winning a BY-ELECTION in March 1969

66 *… there can be no justice while there is a Unionist Party, because while there is a Unionist Party they will, by their gerrymandering, control Northern Ireland and be the government of Northern Ireland.* 99

SOURCE 9 An extract from a sermon given by Ian Paisley in January 1969

66 *The civil rights people don't believe in civil rights at all, they're just a bunch of republican rebels, that's what they are. Let's be very clear about this, they have no time for law and order, they have no time for this country and they mean to destroy this country, and we mean to see that this country will not be destroyed.* 99

SOURCE 10 The loyalist leader Gusty Spence speaking in the 1990s. Spence was the leader of the UVF paramilitary group. He was imprisoned for murder (which he denied) in 1966, and was released in 1983

66 *Civil rights was a Catholic organisation. We were told by all the powers that be that it was dominated by Catholics, and that it certainly was not for us. With hindsight, everyone should have been in the civil rights movement. We should have forced the government to bring forward enlightened policies which would make life better for all. We knew that the Official Unionist Party had opposed at Westminster [in the UK Parliament] every piece of enlightened legislation from the National Health Service right through to Family Allowances and justified that because Catholics have big families and they would get more money and they wouldn't want to work and they would live off the state and all. We actually believed all that rubbish.* 99

SOURCE 11 The view of a Protestant Belfast housewife on the civil rights movement in 1969

66 *It was all the Catholics this, the Catholics that, living in poverty and us lording it over them. People looked around and said, 'What, are they talking about us? With the damp running down the walls and the houses not fit to live in.'* 99

SOURCE 12 From *Ulster's Protestant Working Class*, the report of a series of discussions organised in 1994 by the Springfield Inter-Community Project in Belfast. The aim was to explore how the Protestant working class in Belfast viewed themselves and their history

66 *OK, we stupidly fought the civil rights people every inch of the way, but their demands were eventually all met – they got everything they asked for. If Catholics had been prepared to take one step at a time, we would have had to reach some accommodation with them, but no, nothing was ever good enough, and their insatiable demands and the 'all or nothing' of the IRA has just bred a deep resentment and anger.* 99

SOURCE 13 A civil rights march in Gt James' Street, Londonderry, in the 1960s

■ ACTIVITY

Look at Source 1 on page 72. After seeing shocking scenes like this many people demanded an explanation for the violence. The media led many people outside Northern Ireland to assume that the kind of view expressed in Source 8 was the explanation. However, with the benefit of hindsight we, as historians, can try to put together a bigger picture which includes the violent reaction from Loyalists, but brings in other factors as well.

Use the information and sources on pages 72–77 to examine all the factors and put together your own answer to the question 'Why was the reaction to the civil rights movement so violent?'

Why were British troops sent to Northern Ireland in 1969?

AFTER O'NEILL RESIGNED, the new Northern Ireland Prime Minister was James Chichester-Clark, O'Neill's cousin. He was a middle-of-the-road Unionist much like O'Neill – neither a reformer nor a hardliner – who held a senior position in the party. He inherited a terrible situation.

Tension in Northern Ireland was rising as the summer marching season approached. There was a riot following a march in Dungiven in July, which resulted in the first death in the renewed Troubles.

As the date for the Londonderry Apprentice Boys' march approached, the people of the Catholic Bogside area of Londonderry feared the worst. The most controversial part of the route of the Apprentice Boys' march was along the walls of the city where marchers could look down on the Catholic Bogside and Creggan. There was a long track record of violence, usually between rival loyalist and republican gangs after the march had passed this area. Given the heightened tension in 1969 a march which often created violence in 'normal' times seemed a big risk. The Catholics expected trouble and prepared for it. They barricaded the Bogside.

The power to ban marches lay with the Northern Ireland Home Affairs Minister Robert Porter, who was, of course, a Unionist. The Nationalist leader John Hume asked Porter to ban the Apprentice Boys' march and was refused. Hume then went to the Home Office in London which ignored him and accused him of being alarmist.

1. Why do you think Hume wanted the march banned?
2. Why do you think the request was refused?

The Battle of the Bogside

The parade itself, on 12 August, was relatively peaceful. However, soon after it ended, Protestants and Catholics began to throw missiles at each other after Loyalists threw pennies at the Catholics (a traditional insult). Before long, there was a riot. When the RUC tried to take down a barricade on Rossville Street, the riot turned into a battle. The police faced a hail of missiles and petrol bombs from the Bogside residents. There are two different explanations for the battle. The police say that they attempted to dismantle the barricade because they were trying to get into a better position to separate the mobs. The Catholic version of events is that this was a direct attack by the police, aided by loyalist thugs, on Catholic homes.

Rioting continued for two days, in what became known as the Battle of the Bogside. The police were unable to enter the area. The first of Northern Ireland's 'no-go' areas had been created.

SOURCE 1 From *The Road to Bloody Sunday* by Raymond Maclean

66 *It was just before 7p.m. and a fairly large group of people had gathered at Francis Street and Upper William Street. The majority of people were angry and resentful at the day's parade, but although they felt in some way sympathetic towards the rioters they could not bring themselves to be active participants in this type of action. Just after 7p.m. the police made a major charge right into Rossville Street, and pushed the rioters back towards the Bogside corner. To our amazement, the police were accompanied by a large number of loyalist militants, who started breaking windows in the houses along Rossville Street. The participation of police and loyalist militants in a combined operation was the last straw for the resentful, uncommitted observers in Francis Street, and we all moved off to take up our separate functions, in the full knowledge that this riot was going to be a big one.* 99

SOURCE 2 From *The B-Specials: A History of the Ulster Special Constabulary* by Sir Arthur Hazlett, 1972

66 *The march itself was orderly and passed through the city without trouble, except that a few stones were thrown at the very tail end of it as it passed Waterloo Place. No sooner were the Apprentice Boys in their buses on the way home than serious rioting broke out. It did not take the form of Catholics versus Protestants, but of Catholics versus the RUC, the police trying to prevent the mob breaking out into the main shopping area. The rioting lasted most of the night, the mob using stones and petrol bombs and the RUC using water cannon and later tear gas. There were serious fires in the city and by morning there were 94 police injured as well as 22 civilians. A BBC newsman reported, 'The RUC have been magnificent. It is difficult to explain how they have managed to keep their tempers.' Rioting was not confined to Londonderry, and there were outbreaks in Newry, Strabane and Coalisland.* 99

3. How do Sources 1 and 2 differ in their accounts?
4. What possible explanations are there for these differences?

Intervention from the Republic

At the height of the violence, the Irish Taoiseach Jack Lynch expressed serious concern. He sent Irish Army ambulances to the border (just a few kilometres away) to treat the injured. He also accused the RUC of no longer being an impartial (unbiased) force. The RUC came across very badly in some (but not all) reports of the events (see Sources 1 and 2). In fact, reports varied considerably. Lynch said he intended to intervene in the situation. He called for a United Nations peacekeeping force to be sent in. His words heartened Nationalists, but they alarmed the Northern Ireland government, who regarded his actions as interference. To many Loyalists in Northern Ireland, Lynch's actions simply confirmed suspicions that Northern Ireland was facing a republican plot sponsored by the government of the Republic.

5. Using your work on pages 72–77 explain what effect you think Lynch's announcement had on Protestant opinion.

Troops in

After two days of rioting the RUC officers were exhausted and there seemed to be a danger of the violence spreading further across the Province. The government had little choice but to call in the army. There were troops stationed in Northern Ireland anyway. They seemed the best solution to the problem.

The Battle of the Bogside ended on the afternoon of 14 August. Catholics welcomed the British troops as an impartial force. The soldiers were staggered at the extent of the violence and destruction.

■ TASK

Write a 50-word entry for a historical encyclopaedia on 'The Battle of the Bogside'. You must choose one of these photographs to go with your definition, and explain your choice.

SOURCE 3 Nationalist youths preparing petrol bombs in Lecky Road, Bogside, August 1969

SOURCE 5 The aftermath of the Battle of the Bogside

SOURCE 4 Barricades in Wellington Street, part of the Bogside, August 1969

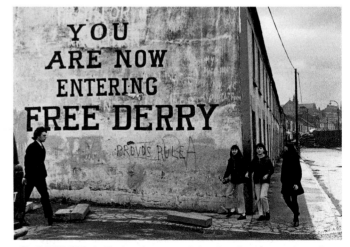

SOURCE 6 Today the area of the riots has been cleared but it is still marked by the famous Free Derry Corner

Troops into Belfast

The violence was not limited to Londonderry. Disturbances soon started in other towns. The most serious violence was in Belfast. Alarmed and angry Protestants, many believing their country was under threat, attacked Catholics in the Falls Road area. Many of the Protestants involved were alleged to be B-Specials. The Catholics fought back. Homes were burned, businesses were destroyed and shots were fired by both sides. In one night six people died, twelve factories burned down and 100 houses were wrecked.

Many Protestants suffered, but it was the Catholics who were most under threat. They were outnumbered by about two to one, and every Catholic area was surrounded by Protestant areas. When Nationalists created disturbances elsewhere in the Province, it was the Catholics of Belfast who faced reprisals – violence, burnings, beatings and shootings – as a result. Over 1800 families were forced out of their homes, usually because they lived in mixed neighbourhoods. About 1500 of the 1800 families forced out were Catholics.

At this point, incorrect RUC intelligence said that an IRA-led uprising was imminent. The RUC called for support from British troops (see Source 9). RUC armoured cars were armed with heavy machine guns. A nine-year-old boy was killed in his bed by one of these weapons as its bullets ripped through the wall of his bedroom. Bernadette Devlin told the British government that if troops were not brought into Belfast too there would be a massacre. On the afternoon of 15 August 1969, the British Army came onto the streets of Belfast. They would still be there 30 years later. Nationalists welcomed the troops as rescuers and gave them tea and sandwiches. There was peace for a short while.

SOURCE 8 Belfast people with belongings they have salvaged after being driven out of their homes

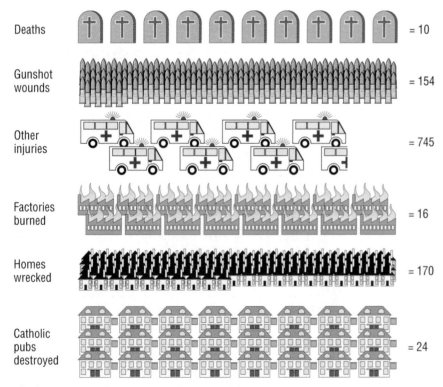

Deaths	= 10
Gunshot wounds	= 154
Other injuries	= 745
Factories burned	= 16
Homes wrecked	= 170
Catholic pubs destroyed	= 24

SOURCE 7 The total casualties of 1969

SOURCE 9 A message from the RUC Inspector General, Anthony Peacocke, to the British government to send in troops with armoured cars, August 1969

66 Information is to hand from a reliable source that an infiltration of members of the Irish Republican Army is about to commence from Eire into Northern Ireland. It is the intention to escalate the degree of control over inward-bound traffic and to this end assistance in the form of patrols by armoured cars is also requested. The information indicates that the infiltrators will be armed and the support of mobile units, which I cannot supply, would be of material assistance in countering these subversive activities against the government and people of Northern Ireland. 99

S OURCE 10 British troops receiving Christmas presents, in 1969

SOURCE 11 A corporal from the Parachute Regiment describing his experiences in 1969

66 *We used to just wander around in pairs like policemen. You'd go out for a two-hour patrol and in two hours you drank twenty cups of tea because everybody wanted to give you a cup of tea and a sandwich. We called it the honeymoon tour. We had a disco every night and the girls used to come in ... That's where a lot of the lads met their wives. Because we were in a predominantly Protestant area we had all Protestants, but down at TAC HQ on Hastings Street, right on the peace line between the Falls and Shankill Roads, they had a big massive disco and used to get women from both sides. Everybody used to mix together. There was no trouble at all.* 99

■ ACTIVITY

Troops Out Now!
As the conflict in Northern Ireland continued, this slogan helped Republicans with their attempts at fundraising, especially in the USA. This is because many Americans thought that Britain had 'occupied' Northern Ireland. Your task is to write a short article for an American newspaper explaining why the British government had to send troops into Northern Ireland in 1969. You should mention:

■ rioting in Londonderry and Belfast
■ exhaustion of the RUC
■ relations between the RUC and nationalist communities
■ how the arrival of troops can be interpreted (or misinterpreted) differently by different groups in Ireland.

■ REVIEW TASK

After the events of 1969, each of the various sides blamed the others for the descent into violence. Your task is to decide whether any one group was responsible, or whether responsibility should be shared.

In this section you have come across a number of key players. In groups, think about the contribution, positive or negative, made by these key players. For each player, consider

■ their action(s) which helped maintain peace and calm
■ their action(s) which made violence likely.

You could then record your findings like this:

Key players	Contribution	Supporting evidence
The NICRA		
The RUC		
The Unionist government		
The media		
Ian Paisley		
People's Democracy		
The British government		
The British Army		

What were the causes and consequences of the re-emergence of the IRA in 1969–71?

THE ARRIVAL OF the British troops brought peace to Northern Ireland, but not for long. By the end of 1969 the efforts of politicians to find a solution were sidelined by the growing violence on the streets. The most serious violence came from the growing conflict between the British Army and a newly re-emerged IRA.

Within months of the British troops arriving a newly formed IRA was armed and ready for action. It established a secure power base and within a short time it was at war with the British Army. Attempts by the Northern Ireland government to crush the IRA seemed to have the opposite effect. It was a far cry from what the organisers of the civil rights movement had in mind. How did it happen?

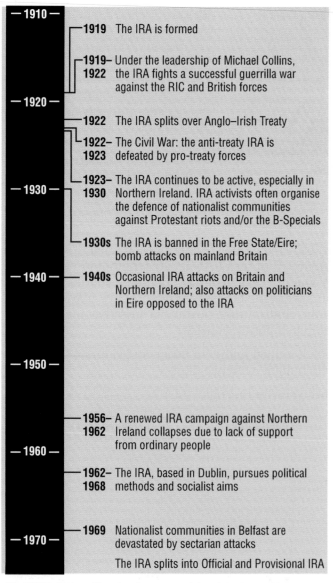

SOURCE 1 The development of the IRA, 1919–69

Stage 1: The Provisional IRA is created

In the early years of Northern Ireland, the IRA had seen itself as the protector of the Catholic nationalist community. After the violence in Belfast in 1969, Catholics nicknamed the IRA the 'I Ran Away'. It had failed dismally to protect the nationalist community.

In December 1969, the movement split and the Provisional IRA, led by Sean MacStiofain, was born. The Provisionals declared themselves once again the defenders of nationalist areas (see Source 3). The Provisionals recruited new members and trained them during the winter of 1970. In back kitchens in Catholic areas such as the Ardoyne, Upper Falls and West Belfast, there were lectures on using and maintaining weapons. The Provisionals received money and weapons from sympathisers in the USA. They also received help from the Republic. The future Taoiseach Charles Haughey was accused of diverting to the Provisionals £30,000 meant for Catholics made homeless by the Troubles.

Stage 2: The British Army become 'the bad guys'

Later in the summer of 1970, the good relations between the British Army and the nationalist community collapsed. The UK government had left the army under the political control of the Unionist government in Stormont. In July, after four Protestants were killed in a gun battle in the Short Strand area of Belfast, the government ordered 3000 troops into the Falls Road to search for weapons and IRA suspects. This was against the advice of the army commander General Freeland. Freeland had also asked for all marches (including Orange marches) to be banned, but his request was turned down. The Lower Falls was swamped with troops. Tear gas was used. The area was put under CURFEW for 35 hours, leaving many people stranded without food. Homes were wrecked as troops searched for arms. The army which had saved the Catholic community from a potential massacre in 1969 now seemed to have turned against them. It was a propaganda gift for the Provisionals.

SOURCE 4 A British soldier watches a Falls Road resident while other troops search his home, July 1970

SOURCE 5 A private in the army describing the effect of the Falls curfew of July 1970

❝ *I felt that I was invading the man's home. I felt guilty and ashamed. The place was saturated with CS [tear] gas. Children were coughing. I'm talking now about toddlers, kids of three, four, five.*

. . . I think the major effect of the Falls curfew was that it gave the community in the Lower Falls the opportunity to see the IRA as their saviours and they saw the British Army as the enemy, a foreign occupying force.

. . . I didn't see myself as a foreign invader and I don't think they did either up until the curfew. ❞

Stage 3: The IRA goes on the attack

Many IRA activists still wanted an armed struggle to rid Ireland of the British invader. To the Provisionals, the Falls curfew and similar actions gave them the justification to go on the attack against both Unionists and the army. In 1971, they launched a major bombing campaign, in which they targeted Protestant shops and businesses. By May 1971, the IRA had set off 136 bombs. They also attacked Catholics if they thought they were disloyal – for example, tarring and feathering girls who went out with British soldiers.

The Provisionals intensified attacks on the army, as well. By the end of 1970, 46 British Army soldiers had been killed, most of them by the Provisional IRA. In March 1971, they lured three soldiers to a party and shot them in the back of the head. On 8 August, one soldier was shot dead and six more

injured. The response to this campaign was more searches by troops. This in turn increased support for the Provisionals – a vicious circle.

In 1971, the Provisionals changed the nature of the conflict: it now became a bitter, no-holds-barred war. They were not just defending their community. They were now attempting to achieve their long-cherished aim of completely removing any British presence from Ireland.

1. Explain why the Provisional IRA had little trouble finding recruits.
2. With hindsight, the Falls curfew and searches were a mistake. Would you say the action was the responsibility of the Stormont government, the UK government or the army? Explain your answer.
3. What do Sources 3–5 suggest are the main reasons why relations between the army and the nationalist community broke down in the early 1970s?

Drawing breath ...

Well done! You have made your way through five chapters of this book, and the last couple have been pretty action packed! Look at what you have covered.

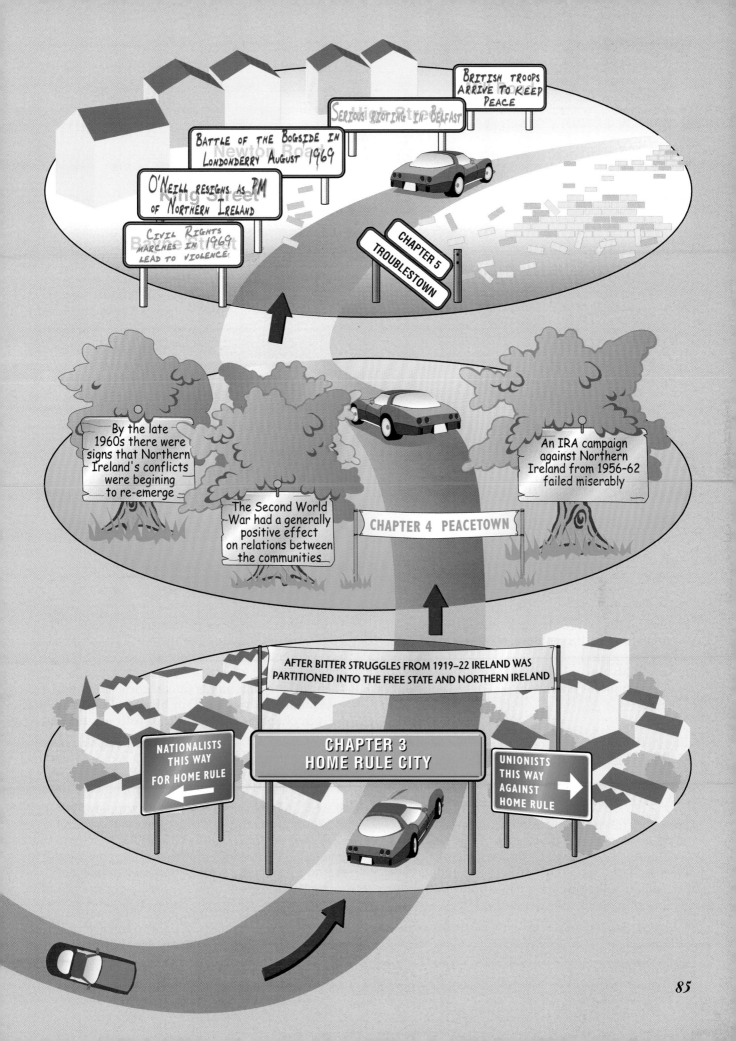

■ REVIEW ACTIVITY Chapters 1–5

Why did violence break out in 1969?

As you know, there are many different explanations of why conflict broke out in 1969 and why it continued for another 30 years. Here are some typical opinions that have been expressed.

> **A.**
> If you want my opinion, the early history is not that important, but I believe the conflict began in the 1880s when the issue of Home Rule created a divided country.

> **B.**
> Surely we only have to go back as far as the formation of the civil rights movement in 1967?

> **C.**
> I don't think you should underestimate the power of history in Ireland – the arguments of 1969 look just the same as the arguments of 1641 to me.

> **D.**
> This conflict is rooted in the late 1960s. Catholics in the civil rights movement wanted to reform the Northern Ireland state, not destroy it. They were not interested in the Boyne, Wolfe Tone or Michael Collins.

> **E.**
> OK, I accept that the conflict in 1969 was between Catholics and Protestants, but they were fighting about twentieth-century issues like civil rights. It was not like the seventeenth century when the conflict really was about religion.

> **F.**
> I think that economic factors are the key reason for the conflict in 1969. The economy was just beginning to struggle in the late 1960s and that had a tradition of causing sectarian conflict.

> **G.**
> I don't think any of this history is important apart from one event – Partition.

> **H.**
> We shouldn't even be looking at the events of 1969, it's the revival of the IRA in 1970 and 1971 that really matters.

> **I.**
> Of course the conflict in 1969 goes back into history. The conflict is about who holds political power in Northern Ireland. That was true in 1969, it was true in 1912, and it was true in the 1500s.

> **J.**
> Aren't we forgetting the British dimension here? A quick look at history shows Britain closely involved in conflict in Ireland from the 1500s, through the seventeenth, eighteenth and nineteenth centuries and up to the present. The 1969 conflict was just another outbreak of conflict between Irish and British.

1. In a small group, look back on your work in chapters 1–5 (there's a quick version on the previous page!).
2. Now study the opinions being expressed in the speech bubbles about why violence broke out in 1969.

3. Sort them into three categories:
a) statements you agree with
b) statements you disagree with
c) statements you can't decide about.
4. For all the statements in categories a) and b) explain why you agree or disagree. Use evidence from chapters 1–5 to back up your arguments.

■ COURSEWORK ASSIGNMENT

Here are two views relating to the question 'Why did violence break out in 1969?'

View 1: 'The conflict in 1969 was the result of increasing tensions building up in the 1960s and eventually triggered off by the civil rights marches.'
View 2: 'The conflict in Northern Ireland in 1969 was simply a continuation of a conflict between rival groups going back many centuries.'

Your task is to explain why each of these views has its supporters.

You need to explain:

■ what evidence and arguments support View 1
■ how convincing you think the evidence and arguments are
■ what evidence and arguments support View 2
■ how convincing you think the evidence and arguments are.

You can add a conclusion, if you wish, explaining whether you personally support one view or whether you feel each view is equally valid.

6 WHY DID ATTEMPTS AT PEACE FAIL IN 1971–93?

Fast track: Northern Ireland, 1971–93

The paramilitaries

The total death toll in the Troubles has been over 3500. Republican paramilitaries were responsible for almost 60 per cent of the killings, loyalists for almost 30 per cent. The remaining ten per cent were either killed by the security forces or by an unknown party. Over half of the victims were innocent civilians with no connections to the paramilitaries or the security forces at all. Throughout the 1970s, 1980s and 1990s, therefore, the paramilitaries have been a very powerful force in Northern Ireland. How were these movements able to cause such devastation without being stopped?

Firstly, both republican and loyalist paramilitaries believed deeply in what they were doing – defending their people and fighting for a cause. They were prepared to kill or be killed for this cause. This made them into formidable organisations.

Both sets of paramilitaries had a bedrock of support in certain areas of Northern Ireland. This support rose and fell, but it never disappeared. (The Republicans also had supporters in the Irish Republic and the USA.) The paramilitaries controlled their own areas of Northern Ireland with an iron grip, using propaganda and intimidation. Few who opposed them dared to do it openly.

The paramilitaries also had political 'wings'. In the early 1980s, Sinn Fein became an important political force in Northern Ireland, despite its support for the IRA's violent campaigns. A decade later, parties such as the Progressive Unionist Party emerged as representatives of loyalist paramilitary groups.

These political 'wings' gave the paramilitaries additional influence. It meant that it was much easier to have discussions with legitimate politicians. It also opened up a way for people who felt that the existing parties did not properly represent them to express their views; for example many Nationalists supported Sinn Fein because they felt that the SDLP did not represent them, not because they sympathised with the IRA.

The politicians

Despite their power, the paramilitaries were supported by only a small minority of people in Northern Ireland. The majority voted for democratic political parties. Most Catholics voted for the Social and Democratic Labour Party (SDLP), a democratic nationalist party formed in 1970. Most Protestants supported the Ulster Unionist Party, the largest political party in Northern Ireland. The voters entrusted these parties with the responsibility of working out solutions to Northern Ireland's problems.

Politicians often get the blame for their failure to end the violence. This is not very fair, since they were not the ones who were planting bombs or shooting people. However, it is also true to say that all the political initiatives of the 1970s and 1980s failed to end the conflict. The politicians had many conferences and talks, but at the time most of them seemed to be pointless, always ending in bitter disagreement. The question observers asked was whether the politicians were part of the problem or part of the solution. It was not until the 1990s that the politicians began to make real progress.

■ TASK

Look at the graph of Troubles-related deaths in Source 1 and the events in the timeline (Source 2). Politicians in Northern Ireland, Britain and the Republic were often accused of simply reacting to increases in violence rather than trying to solve the problems. Does the information here support that view? Discuss this question in your class.

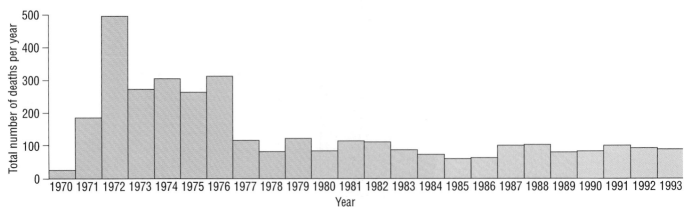

SOURCE 1 Deaths per year in the Troubles

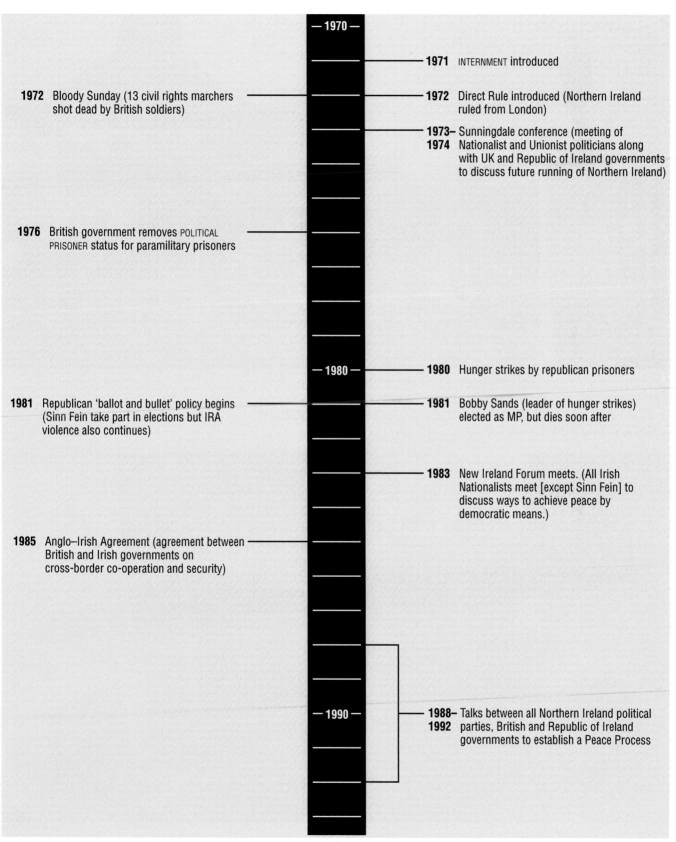

1972 Bloody Sunday (13 civil rights marchers shot dead by British soldiers)

1976 British government removes POLITICAL PRISONER status for paramilitary prisoners

1981 Republican 'ballot and bullet' policy begins (Sinn Fein take part in elections but IRA violence also continues)

1985 Anglo–Irish Agreement (agreement between British and Irish governments on cross-border co-operation and security)

— 1970 —

— 1980 —

— 1990 —

1971 INTERNMENT introduced

1972 Direct Rule introduced (Northern Ireland ruled from London)

1973– Sunningdale conference (meeting of
1974 Nationalist and Unionist politicians along with UK and Republic of Ireland governments to discuss future running of Northern Ireland)

1980 Hunger strikes by republican prisoners

1981 Bobby Sands (leader of hunger strikes) elected as MP, but dies soon after

1983 New Ireland Forum meets. (All Irish Nationalists meet [except Sinn Fein] to discuss ways to achieve peace by democratic means.)

1988– Talks between all Northern Ireland political
1992 parties, British and Republic of Ireland governments to establish a Peace Process

SOURCE 2 Timeline 1970–93

What made the paramilitaries so powerful?

SOURCE 1 The scene in Enniskillen after an IRA bomb went off at a Remembrance Day service in 1987, killing eleven people and seriously injuring over 60 more. The bomb caused outrage and seriously damaged support for the IRA, especially in the USA

SOURCE 2 The shattered interior of a bar in Loughinisland, County Down, in 1994. Loyalist paramilitaries shot dead six Catholics watching a football match in the bar. It was part of a series of tit-for-tat paramilitary killings in the early 1990s

Sources 1 and 2 give some idea of the type of acts carried out by the paramilitaries during the Troubles. Most of the violence took place in Northern Ireland, but there were also attacks in the Republic and in mainland Britain. Bombs caused the greatest devastation, but there were many other kinds of violence, too. There were countless shootings and beatings. There was intimidation as well as murder. Thousands of Protestants and Catholics living in areas where they were in the minority were hounded out of their homes. In rural areas, Protestants and Catholics lived with the constant fear of attack.

A huge range of measures was used to try to defeat the paramilitaries. The RUC was the main security force. There were also thousands of regular British soldiers, as well as thousands more part-time soldiers in the Ulster Defence Regiment (UDR). The security forces also used informers and the military intelligence services to discover information. In the areas near the border with the Republic of Ireland, there was a sophisticated and brutal conflict between the IRA and the army's elite SAS regiment.

Despite these formidable enemies, and despite the misery they caused to so many people, republican and loyalist paramilitaries remained powerful organisations throughout the 1970s, 1980s and 1990s. In this investigation we examine why.

What did the paramilitaries stand for?

Republicans

We want a 32-county Republic of Ireland with no political involvement with Britain at all.

We are the defenders of nationalist communities from the violence of Loyalists, the British Army and the RUC.

We have the right to use armed force against the British forces who occupy our country.

We are part of a tradition which goes back to 1916 and even further.

Loyalists

We want Northern Ireland to remain part of the United Kingdom, and we want to defend our Protestant religion.

We are the defenders of our communities and people from republican paramilitaries like the IRA.

We have the right to use force against enemies who attack our people and our state.

We are part of a tradition which goes back to 1912 and even further.

■ TASK

In small groups, discuss these questions.

1. The speech bubbles summarise how the paramilitaries saw themselves. How do you think they were seen by
a) people in Britain
b) ordinary people in Northern Ireland who did not support them?

2. Both sides claim to be part of a tradition going back at least as far as the early twentieth century. How are they similar to or different from the Republicans and Loyalists of the early twentieth century? (You may need to look back to your work from Chapter 3 to remind yourself.)

3. In what ways do the two sets of paramilitaries appear to be similar to each other?

What was the effect of internment?

In August 1971, the Northern Ireland Prime Minister Brian Faulkner introduced internment, under Northern Ireland's Special Powers Act. Internment meant that anyone the security forces suspected of terrorism could be arrested and held in prison without being charged or put on trial. It was Faulkner's attempt to cripple the IRA. It had been used very effectively against the IRA in 1956–62, but this time it was a disastrous failure. There were a number of reasons for this:

- **The RUC's intelligence was badly out of date.** This meant that the people who were targeted were often no longer active. Between August 1971 and February 1972 1600 out of 2357 internees were released. Crucially, none of the new IRA leaders were arrested.
- **Internment was only used against Nationalists.** Every suspect rounded up was a Nationalist or Republican – no attempt was made to arrest loyalist paramilitaries.
- **It increased support for the IRA in the USA.** The decision to introduce internment caused outrage in the USA and the Republic. This almost certainly helped the IRA to raise funds abroad and to obtain weapons from the USA (see page 123).
- **It was linked to violence.** A substantial number of those interned were interrogated using violence and torture. This was confirmed by the Compton Commission (a government report). In the early 1980s, the European Commission on Human Rights condemned the treatment of prisoners in Northern Ireland.

Instead of crippling the IRA, internment boosted its support. As a direct response, residents of Londonderry and Belfast set up barricades with the help of IRA activists. The barricades kept out loyalist attackers, and the districts within them soon became 'no-go' areas, even for the security forces. This enabled the IRA to make more bombs, train more activists and so increase its attacks on soldiers. In some areas, the troops lost their discipline and beat suspects or smashed up houses. This was a gift for the IRA's propaganda machine and just increased support for the IRA still further.

SOURCE 3 An extract from *The Politics of Irish Freedom* by Sinn Fein leader Gerry Adams

66 *Support for the IRA amongst the nationalist population of the Six Counties has been ... the sea in which the people's army [the IRA] has swum and, like the sea, it has its tides, its ebbs and flows, but it is always there. The nationalist people withdrew their consent to being ruled by Stormont ... and proceeded, in succeeding years, to make the Six Counties ungovernable, even in an environment of British military saturation of nationalist areas.* 99

1. Is it fair to say internment did more harm than good? Explain your answer.
2. How reliable would you consider Source 3 to be as a view on support for the IRA? Explain your answer.
3. Explain how Source 4 could be used to increase support for the IRA.

SOURCE 4 British troops round up suspects under the internment laws, 1971

Bloody Sunday

In Londonderry on Sunday 30 January 1972, there was a huge protest march against internment, organised by the civil rights movement. Fifteen thousand people defied a ban on marches and gathered in the centre of the city. Troops of the Parachute Regiment sealed off the area, and were met with a hail of stones thrown by youths. There is a lot of confusion over the sequence of events that followed. The soldiers say that they were fired on and returned fire. The result was that thirteen marchers, all apparently unarmed, were killed. Some of them were shot in the back.

The inquiry which followed was headed by Lord Widgery. It criticised the shooting by the troops as 'bordering on the reckless', but no action was taken against any soldiers. The report accepted the army's version of events, that the soldiers had been fired on first by IRA gunmen. To Nationalists, it was a whitewash, a cover-up. The controversy was still raging 26 years later, in January 1998, when the British Prime Minister Tony Blair announced a new inquiry into the events.

Bloody Sunday was tragic for those involved. Its importance in terms of the conflict lay in how it affected views and attitudes. It was a propaganda victory for the Republicans. The reaction outside the UK was one of outrage. Funding for the IRA from the USA increased. In Dublin, the British Embassy was burned down. These events also strengthened the argument of the hardline Republicans that defending their communities was no longer enough. They said that the IRA had to go on the attack to get the British out of Ireland.

SOURCE 6 A mural in Londonderry today commemorating Bloody Sunday

SOURCE 5 Extract from *Provos* by Peter Taylor, a journalist with a lifetime's experience of reporting on Northern Ireland

66 *To this day, it is difficult to convince Nationalists in the city that the killing of their fellow citizens was anything other than premeditated murder by the army, authorised by Stormont and the British Government. How else, they ask, would soldiers slaughter thirteen innocent people taking part in a peaceful anti-internment march? The only explanation that makes sense to them, and there remain few voices to the contrary, is that there were orders from on high to teach the rebels of 'Free Derry' a lesson they would never forget. This lesson, as the evidence of their eyes told them, was to send a good number of the marchers back home in boxes. After much research, I do not believe this 'conspiracy' theory to be true. 'Bloody Sunday' was a dreadful mistake and should never have happened, but there were no orders or directives from on high instructing the paratroopers to do what they did. But 'Bloody Sunday' cannot be seen in isolation. It was a tragedy waiting to happen. For many months there had been endless rioting in the city. Every day, at tea time, there would be a confrontation at the corner of William Street and Rossville Street between soldiers guarding the entrance to the city centre and the rioters operating out of 'Free Derry'. Day after day soldiers would stand there being pelted by rioters and the stone throwers would get in plenty of practice. The junction was known, with good reason, as 'aggro corner'.* 99

SOURCE 7 SDLP politician John Hume's reaction to Bloody Sunday, 1972

66 *Many people down there in the Bogside now feel that it is a united Ireland or nothing.* 99

4. List the different reactions to Bloody Sunday and explain those reactions.
5. Explain how Bloody Sunday helped the IRA in terms of
a) practical help
b) discrediting its opponents.

Loyalist paramilitaries

In the early years of the conflict, the loyalist paramilitaries simply reacted to the violence of the IRA. As the IRA's violence increased in the 1970s, Loyalists in areas such as the Shankill in Belfast and the Fountains in Londonderry became increasingly concerned. In September 1971, a loyalist paramilitary organisation, the Ulster Defence Association, was formed as a response to the threat of the IRA. During the 1970s and 1980s, the UDA and other loyalist paramilitaries (such as the Ulster Defence Force – the UDF, and Ulster Freedom Fighters – the UFF) simply responded to republican violence by killing ordinary Catholics.

> **SOURCE 8** Charles Harding Smith, one of the founding members of the UFF, a paramilitary group founded in 1973. This extract is from an interview for a TV series on Loyalists broadcast in 1999
>
> 66 **Interviewer:** *But most of the killings that the UFF carried out were not against the IRA, they were against innocent Catholics.*
>
> **Charles Harding Smith:** *I think at the start of the campaign the view was that the IRA had full support within their communities and therefore it was felt that in order to put pressure on the IRA, the same effect would be achieved by conducting a campaign against the communities where the IRA found its support.* 99

6. Source 8 agrees with Source 3 that the IRA had the support of the nationalist community. Does this strike you as strange? Explain your answer.
7. You have seen several times that ignorance has played a key role in the conflict in Northern Ireland. How does Source 8 support this view?

By the early 1990s, the loyalist paramilitaries had begun to take the initiative and were matching the IRA's level of violence. They now attacked IRA and Sinn Fein activists as well as civilians in the belief that if the violence escalated far enough people would call a halt. It was all part of a vicious circle which was to continue well into the 1990s. The threat of the IRA generated support for loyalist paramilitaries. Loyalist attacks reinforced the role of the IRA as defenders of their community. Some people have even said that the paramilitaries relied on each other to give themselves a reason to exist (see Sources 9 and 14).

8. What point is the cartoonist making about the paramilitaries in Source 9?

■ TASK A

The effect of paramilitary violence in the Troubles can be described as a vicious circle. Draw a diagram to show this idea.

SOURCE 9 A cartoon which appeared in *The Times* newspaper in April 1999. At the time of the cartoon, the peace process which was taking place was being threatened by the fact that neither the IRA nor the main loyalist paramilitary groups would decommission (give up) their arms

Economic factors

The paramilitaries thrived on poverty. Their support generally came from the more economically deprived areas.

Northern Ireland's economy was already in trouble in the 1970s, and the Troubles made this worse: businesses were wrecked by bombs, and foreign firms were reluctant to set up factories or offices there. These problems continued well into the 1980s and 1990s. Sources 10 and 11 give some idea of the poverty and hardship in Northern Ireland in this period.

The young unemployed of both communities were an easy target for recruitment to the paramilitaries. In nationalist areas, it was not hard to convince some young men that Protestant discrimination kept them unemployed. The IRA would mention a few examples of Protestant oppression going back to the Plantation – just the bits of history which suited them – and they soon had a volunteer. A similar process applied in loyalist areas, with different interpretations of the events, of course.

Sectarian violence was largely confined to the poorer areas, where the members of the paramilitaries lived. The more prosperous areas suffered far less damage and fewer than half as many deaths as the deprived areas (see Source 12).

1980–81

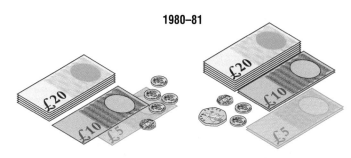

Northern Ireland £119.20   England £152.70

1994–95

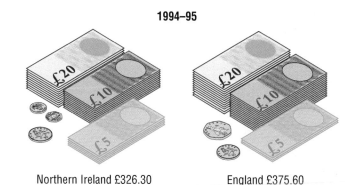

Northern Ireland £326.30   England £375.60

SOURCE 10 Weekly household income (£), 1980–81 and 1994–95

SOURCE 11 Dependence on state welfare benefits in Northern Ireland (per cent)

	1985–87			1988–90/91		
	Catholic	Protestant	Overall	Catholic	Protestant	Overall
Percentage of population receiving benefits	43	24	30	35	19	23

Average death rate:

In five wealthiest electoral wards

 per 1000 population

In five most deprived electoral wards

 per 1000 population

SOURCE 12 Troubles-related deaths in prosperous and deprived areas of Northern Ireland. This data comes from a project run by the University of Ulster. You can find out more from its website at http://www.incore.ulst.ac.uk/

SOURCE 13 An extract from a research project on Northern Ireland called *Intimidation and the Control of Conflict*, 1986

❝ The business and professional contacts we spoke to suggested that the middle classes were more likely to support co-operation ... They are more likely to live in religiously integrated districts, and they are more conscious of the threat presented to the business life of the town [Belfast] by civil disorder. ❞

■ TASK B

Go back to your vicious circle diagram from Task A on page 94. Amend it to show how these economic factors would affect the situation.

How did the paramilitaries keep control?

It has always been very difficult to be sure exactly how much support there really was for the loyalist or republican paramilitaries. Many people probably agreed with the views in Source 14, but few people expressed opinions like this if they lived in areas where the paramilitaries were strong. The paramilitaries kept a firm grip in the areas they controlled. During the Troubles, many housing estates that had been socially and culturally mixed became wholly nationalist or loyalist. Those people who could moved out to less troubled areas. Many were forced out of areas where they belonged to the minority group.

The paramilitaries ruled through fear. Some people who did not support the use of violence were intimidated into silence, or even forced to help in paramilitary activities. Many families in Northern Ireland were held at gunpoint while a paramilitary sniper used one of their bedroom windows for an attack, or were held hostage while one member was forced to drive a car bomb into position.

9. Source 14 comes from a novel. Does this mean it is of no value to the historian?
10. To what extent do the other sources in this section confirm or contradict the view in Source 14?

SOURCE 14 An extract from a novel, *Lies of Silence*, by the Northern Ireland writer Brian Moore. In the novel, a married couple are held hostage by the IRA. The husband is forced to drive his car through security checks with a bomb in the boot, or his wife will be killed. Eventually he is killed by the IRA. This extract shows the woman clashing with the IRA activists

66 *If there was a vote tomorrow among the Catholics of Northern Ireland you wouldn't get five per cent of it. You're just a bunch of crooks, IRA or UDA, Protestants or Catholics, you're all in the same business. Racketeers, the bunch of you. There isn't a building site in this city or a pub that you or the UDA don't hold up for protection money … You've made this place into a shambles and if it was handed over to your crowd tomorrow you wouldn't have the first notion of what to do with it …*

You're not fighting for anybody's freedom. Not mine, not the people of Northern Ireland, not anybody's. The only thing you're doing is making people hate each other worse than ever. Maybe that's what you want, isn't it? Because if the Catholics here stopped hating the Prods, where would the IRA be? 99

SOURCE 15 A Provisional IRA checkpoint. These checkpoints were totally illegal. They existed primarily to maintain a high profile for the IRA

11. Look at Source 15. Scenes like this were interpreted in different ways by different people.

   ■ The IRA argued that their checkpoints reassured people in their communities that the IRA was protecting them.
   ■ Critics said that the checkpoints were more about controlling and intimidating their own people than about protecting them.

   How would a historian find out which interpretation was more accurate?

SOURCE 16 From the loyalist news sheet *Ulster Constitution*, January 1973

66 *A number of persons have been using the 'robot phone' [an answering machine run by the security services which allows people to leave information] in order to tip off the security forces to loyalist arms caches. We warn these people that this is treason and will, if detected, be punished by the usual sentence for this crime.* 99

12. Why do you think that Source 16 uses the phrases 'this is treason' and 'the usual sentence'?

SOURCE 17 The *Irish Republican Information Service*, November 1974, explaining the disappearance of two men from a nationalist housing estate in Belfast

66 *Both men divulged a large amount of information, including the names and addresses of paid informers operating in Derry. Last night both men were executed.* 99

13. Why do you think that Source 17 uses the phrases 'paid informers' and 'executed'?
14. Explain how each of Sources 14 to 17 would be regarded by:

   ■ loyalist paramilitaries
   ■ republican paramilitaries
   ■ residents living in housing estates in Northern Ireland who do not support the paramilitaries.

■ TASK

The Troubles were about propaganda as well as violence.

   Here are some phrases that could be used as captions or slogans:

   ■ Your protectors
   ■ Defending your community

   ■ Beware of the enemy
   ■ Look what they have done to us

Divide into groups of four and choose one phrase each. Now look at Sources 1–17. Decide whether your phrase could be used with each source. Discuss your findings with the rest of your group.

■ ACTIVITY

On pages 90–97, we looked at the factors that kept the paramilitaries strong during the Troubles. How far is each of the statements below supported by the information and sources on pages 90–97? Write a short paragraph about each statement.

   ■ The paramilitaries had ideals they believed in and most people shared those ideals.
   ■ The paramilitaries ruled people by fear.
   ■ The paramilitaries represented and defended the people of their communities.
   ■ Support for the paramilitaries was connected with economic hardship.

   ■ The influence of the paramilitaries made sectarian divisions worse.
   ■ Politicians and the army allowed the paramilitaries to become powerful (without intending to).

Remember to take care when using the sources. There may be evidence in a source to support a statement, but the source may not be completely reliable for the purpose for which you are using it. If you have any doubts, you should explain these doubts in your answer.

Why did Sinn Fein become a significant political force?

■ ACTIVITY

You are a civil servant in Northern Ireland. A senior British minister is coming over on a fact-finding tour. The minister knows very little about Northern Ireland. Prepare a short briefing for the minister on Sinn Fein. You should mention

■ its policies and beliefs
■ its attitude to the IRA and violence
■ its attitude to the British government
■ the main factors which explain its support.

SINN FEIN IS the political wing of the republican movement. It is technically separate from the IRA, but the links between them are very close. Until the mid-1990s Sinn Fein was an uncompromising republican party. It believed in a united Ireland with no links to Britain at all. It also believed that the IRA had the right to use armed force to achieve this aim.

However, for most of the 1970s, Sinn Fein was a relatively unimportant part of the republican movement. The Provisional IRA leaders believed wholeheartedly in the armed struggle, rather than in fighting election campaigns. Since 1969, Sinn Fein had not even put up candidates for local or national elections. In the early 1980s, this changed.

IRA hunger strikes, 1980–81

The IRA hunger strikes played a key role in this process. In 1980 and 1981, republican prisoners in the Maze prison went on hunger strike, demanding to be treated as political prisoners rather than as ordinary criminals. In the rest of the UK, most people supported Prime Minister Margaret Thatcher's determination to give no concessions. However, many Nationalists, even those who did not support IRA violence, sympathised with the strikers and thought that Thatcher was making no effort. They were concerned that justice was not always done. Many Nationalists pointed to the inconsistencies in a system which regarded suspects as mere criminals, but responded to these mere criminals with juryless courts and a large military presence (see Source 1). They felt that the hunger strikes were a HUMANITARIAN issue, and that the actions of the British government were cruel and unreasonable; that British policies were an attempt to crush *all* Nationalists and shut them up.

In April 1981, the hunger striker Bobby Sands was elected as MP for Fermanagh and South Tyrone in a by-election following the death of the previous incumbent, Independent MP Frank Maguire. Sands was a senior IRA commander. His family had been burned out of their home in 1972 and he had been a member of the IRA since he was 18. He had been in prison since 1976, for possession of explosives with intent to use them. By 1980 he was the most senior IRA prisoner. Against the wishes of the IRA leaders outside the Maze, he initiated the second set of hunger strikes in 1981. Hunger strikes had always had a major propaganda impact in Ireland, if less so in Britain.

Technically, Sands actually stood as an independent candidate but Sinn Fein used his victory to great effect. The hunger strikes showed how non-violent action could generate enormous public attention, generally positive rather than the negative publicity which bombs attracted. Sinn Fein saw how successful a political battle could be.

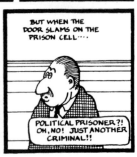

SOURCE 1 A cartoon from *Republican News*, published in Belfast, in June 1980. (Diplock courts did not have juries, because of the problem in Northern Ireland of witnesses being intimidated. The case was tried by the judge)

When Sands died a few months after the election, around 100,000 people (about twenty per cent of the Catholic population of Northern Ireland) attended his funeral. Ten more hunger strikers also died, and their funerals were similarly spectacular events.

From 1981 onwards, Sinn Fein began to campaign actively in elections. After Bobby Sands died in May 1981, his election agent Owen Carron was elected to Westminster as a Sinn Fein MP. In October 1982 Sinn Fein gained ten per cent of the vote in Northern Ireland local elections. In the general election of June 1983, Sinn Fein leader Gerry Adams won the West Belfast seat with 73 per cent of the vote in that constituency. Across the whole of the province, Sinn Fein picked up 13.4 per cent of the vote.

SOURCE 2 Bobby Sands' funeral, May 1981

1. Look at Source 1. What does the source tell historians about nationalist attitudes towards the justice system in Northern Ireland?
2. Look at Source 2. Which of the interpretations below best explains the thousands of mourners attending Sands' funeral?

   ■ 'Vast numbers of Catholics supported Sands, the IRA and Sinn Fein.'
   ■ 'It was a protest against British policy rather than support for the IRA.'

3. How might a) a British politician, or b) a member of a loyalist paramilitary group view Source 3?

SOURCE 3 Danny Morrison, Sinn Fein's public relations officer, in November 1981. After this speech, republican policy was often called the 'Armalite and ballot box' policy. (An Armalite was a rifle favoured by IRA snipers)

66 *Who here really believes that we can win the war through the ballot box? But will anyone here object if with a ballot box in this hand and an Armalite in this hand we take power?* 99

What was the appeal of Sinn Fein?

- Sinn Fein had a reliable base of support in republican areas like South Armagh.
- Unionist politicians demanded tougher security measures to crush Sinn Fein and the IRA. However, without some attempt to improve economic and political conditions for working-class Catholics, tougher security made them more likely to support Sinn Fein.
- The early 1980s were a period of economic recession and high unemployment (there was over 50 per cent unemployment in some areas). The moderate SDLP seemed to be a middle-class party doing little to help working-class Nationalists with their problems.
- Many felt disillusioned with the Catholic Church's attitude. It condemned republicanism but seemed to do little to actually help people suffering poverty and unemployment.
- Sinn Fein used a powerful combination of anti-British statements, republican aims and demands for improved social conditions to gain support. It established centres to advise people on housing and welfare rights.

SOURCE 4 Extracts from *Ourselves Alone? Voices from Belfast's Nationalist Working Class*, published by the Falls Think Tank

66 *We had little faith in the Catholic middle class, for we never expected anything from them. For any working-class section of our community to expect anything from the middle class is stupid anyway.*

. . . We were let down by the South, too: we had the likes of Jack Lynch come out with his 'We will not stand idly by' speech and yet that's exactly what he did . . .

. . . When the violence started, our community was let down by two different groups of people – the IRA and the Church. In the end the IRA came through, but the Church never did. 99

SOURCE 5 A Sinn Fein mural in Beechmount Avenue, Belfast, 1983

SOURCE 6 The Christmas edition of *An Phoblacht*, 1982. The gun at the centre of the Christmas tree is an Armalite rifle

4. Look closely at Sources 4–6. How do they help to explain the increasing support for Sinn Fein in the early 1980s?

SOURCE 7 Sinn Fein leader Gerry Adams speaking in 1983

" I would like to elaborate on Sinn Fein's attitude to armed struggle. Armed struggle is a necessary and morally correct form of resistance in the Six Counties against a government whose presence is rejected by the vast majority of the Irish people . . . There are those who tell us that the British government will not be moved by armed struggle. As has been said before, the history of Ireland and of British colonial involvement throughout the world tells us that they will not be moved by anything else. "

Reactions to the rise of Sinn Fein

For the politicians in Northern Ireland, the Republic and Britain, the increasing support for Sinn Fein was a major worry. If support continued to grow, it looked quite possible that a political party committed to armed struggle would become the largest nationalist party in Northern Ireland. Sources 7–9 make it clear why this was such a concern. There had been no major political initiatives in Northern Ireland since the Power Sharing Executive (see page 103) failed in 1974. Where would that leave democratic politics? What could the politicians do now?

SOURCE 8 Extract from *The Politics of Irish Freedom*, written by Gerry Adams in 1986 and updated in 1994

" In practice, people have been demanding peace since long before the IRA became active. In my own area of Ballymurphy, community groups have long demanded employment, decent housing, play centres, facilities for the aged, handicapped and young . . . Those demands for the kind of peace which is based on justice and equality were made year after year, and year after year they were refused. We cannot have justice and peace in Ireland, because we do not have a society capable of upholding them. "

SOURCE 9 The reaction of British Northern Ireland Secretary Peter Brooke to the election of Gerry Adams as MP for West Belfast in 1983. Adams refused to take his seat in the Westminster Parliament because he would not swear an oath of loyalty to the British state and the Queen

" My reaction was almost one of despair, that they were going to elect someone whom we considered to be a terrorist and who was not going to play any part at Westminster. I had no doubts at all that he belonged to the Provisional IRA. I think he summed up the Armalite and the Ballot Box completely. What a waste the whole thing was. "

5. Read Sources 7–9. Explain why these statements would cause concern to politicians in Northern Ireland, the Republic and Britain.

Did political initiatives achieve anything in this period?

Parties and politicians

During the Troubles, the media reports of bombs and shootings gave people outside Northern Ireland the impression that Northern Ireland was a war zone. It seemed to have no normal life and no normal politics either. This was not the case. There were 'normal' political parties in Northern Ireland, and most people supported them. All the parties had views and policies relating to a wide range of 'normal' issues such as education, health care and housing. However, the key question for all the political parties was clear: how could they bring peace back to Northern Ireland?

Part of the problem for the politicians was that they did not agree on how to do this.

Reactions to political initiatives

Pages 103–107 set out the viewpoints of Northern Ireland's four main political parties on achieving peace in Northern Ireland.

> What we have to do is defeat the IRA. To do this, we'll need a huge security effort.

> We support tough security. Some political reform is needed, but the Irish Republic must *not* be involved in the process.

> We want reform in Northern Ireland. The Republic ought to have some influence on how Northern Ireland is run. As a minority, we feel we need the Republic's protection.

> The only way to solve our problems is to cut all connections with Britain.

Hardline Unionist e.g. DUP

Moderate Unionist e.g. UUP

Moderate Nationalist e.g. SDLP

Hardline Nationalist e.g. Sinn Fein

■ ACTIVITY

Work in small groups. Choose one of the political parties opposite. As you read pages 103–107, write a short press release explaining your party's reaction to

a) the collapse of Power Sharing in 1972 (page 103)
b) the Anglo–Irish Agreement (pages 104–105)
c) the Downing Street Declaration (pages 106–107).

Include a snappy headline which could be used in a newspaper that supports your view.

Northern Ireland's main democratic parties

■ **Ulster Unionist Party:** *Throughout the Troubles, the Ulster Unionist Party was the largest party in Northern Ireland. Most moderate Protestants supported it. Its main aim was to defend Northern Ireland's position as part of the United Kingdom. Its leaders in this period were Brian Faulkner (1971–74), Harry West (1974–79) and James Molyneux (1979–95).*

■ **Democratic Unionist Party (DUP):** *This party emerged in 1971 as a more hardline unionist (or loyalist) party. It was led by Ian Paisley. Its support came mainly from working-class Protestants.*

■ **Alliance Party:** *This was a moderate unionist party founded in April 1970. It wanted to promote reform and reconciliation in Northern Ireland. Its main support came from the middle classes, both Protestant and Catholic.*

■ **Social and Democratic Labour Party (SDLP):** *A combination of Liberal and Labour politicians, along with some of Northern Ireland's socialists, formed this party in August 1970. It was supported by the majority of Catholics and Nationalists, especially the middle classes. Its first leader was Labour politician Gerry Fitt (a socialist and a nationalist). Fitt left the party in 1979 because he felt that it was too nationalist and not socialist enough. John Hume took over as leader.*

Direct Rule

Politicians in the British government in London also had their own solutions. In March 1972, the British government's response to increasing violence in Northern Ireland was to introduce Direct Rule. This meant that the province was run by a British government minister, the Northern Ireland Secretary. It was meant to be a temporary measure while a political solution was found that everyone in Northern Ireland could accept. Direct Rule actually lasted for over 25 years.

During that time, the politicians did not give up. There were three major political initiatives in the period 1973–93.

Attempt 1: The Power-Sharing Executive and the Sunningdale Agreement, 1973–74

- *This was proposed by Northern Ireland Secretary William Whitelaw in consultation with the main Northern Ireland parties.*
- *A new Assembly was elected to govern Northern Ireland.*
- *The main parties in the Assembly were represented on a Power-Sharing Executive (a government which would guarantee to share power between nationalist and unionist communities).*
- *A Council for Ireland was set up which would link Belfast, Dublin and London over issues of concern to all of them. Details of this Council were worked out between the Northern Ireland parties and the British and Irish governments in the Sunningdale Agreement of December 1973.*

The aim of the Power-Sharing Executive was to undermine support for the IRA by giving the nationalist community a say in how Northern Ireland was run. It was made up of six Unionist ministers, four SDLP ministers and one from the Alliance Party. The Executive was elected in 1973 and began governing in 1974.

There were many tensions between the parties. The SDLP agreed to take part in the new Assembly even though it was extremely unhappy that the policy of internment was still in force (see page 92). However, the Nationalists were happy with the idea of a Council of Ireland. They hoped it would give the Republic some say in how Northern Ireland was run. This was exactly what worried most Unionists. They felt that a Council of Ireland would be like letting the government of France interfere in the affairs of an English county such as Kent.

1. Imagine you are reading the *Observer* in November 1973 and someone asks you what the cartoon (Source 1) means. Explain it to them.

The defeat of Power Sharing

It was unionist suspicion about the Council of Ireland which brought down the Power-Sharing Executive. In May 1974, a group calling itself the Ulster Workers Council declared a general strike to protest about the Council of Ireland. There was little support for the strike at first, but loyalist paramilitaries used intimidation to force people to join it. Over the next two weeks, support for the strike increased among the unionist population, bringing Northern Ireland to a halt. Faulkner and the Executive resigned on 27 May. Power Sharing had been defeated and Northern Ireland was back under Direct Rule.

SOURCE 1 A cartoon from the *Observer* newspaper in November 1973, commenting on the Power-Sharing Executive. The man creeping away from the house of cards is the British Northern Ireland Secretary William Whitelaw. Note the labels on the winds which are about to blow on the Executive

Attempt 2: The Anglo–Irish Agreement, 1985

- *This was agreed between Prime Minister Margaret Thatcher and Irish Taoiseach Garrett Fitzgerald.*
- *It set up an Intergovernmental Conference: the Northern Ireland Secretary and Irish Foreign Minister would meet regularly.*
- *There would be cross-border co-operation on security, legal and political issues.*
- *The Agreement set up its own civil service with staff from both sides of the border.*
- *The British government accepted that there might one day be a united Ireland, but only with the consent of the majority in Northern Ireland.*
- *The Irish government accepted the existence of Partition, and also the principle of consent.*

After Power Sharing, there were no new political initiatives in Northern Ireland until the early 1980s. Between 1980 and 1984, the British Prime Minister Margaret Thatcher held regular meetings with Taoiseachs Charles Haughey and then Garrett Fitzgerald. Both governments were concerned about continuing IRA violence (Mrs Thatcher was almost killed by an IRA bomb in 1984) and about the increasing support for the IRA's political wing, Sinn Fein (see pages 98–101). By 1984, Mrs Thatcher was convinced that any solution to Northern Ireland's conflict would have to involve the Irish Republic in some way. Unionists in Northern Ireland became increasingly concerned during these discussions, but Thatcher ignored their fears. In November 1985, she signed the Anglo–Irish Agreement with Garrett Fitzgerald.

The Agreement was well received in most of mainland Britain and the Republic. In Northern Ireland, the Alliance and SDLP felt that it had possibilities. Sinn Fein rejected it because it effectively confirmed the Partition of Ireland. Unionists and Loyalists in Northern Ireland were united in outrage and opposition to the Agreement. A vast crowd gathered to hear Ian Paisley and James Molyneaux (leader of the Ulster Unionists) condemn it. Unionists felt betrayed: as they saw it, Dublin had been given a say in the running of their province without them even being consulted.

The unionist parties tried every method of CONSTITUTIONAL protest against the Agreement. All fifteen Unionist MPs resigned their seats. There were strikes and demonstrations, some leading to clashes between loyalist paramilitaries and the RUC. Ian Paisley tried to recreate the spirit of opposition to Home Rule under Carson in 1912–14 (see pages 38–40).

Mrs Thatcher largely ignored the protests. Unlike in 1912, this time there was little sympathy for the unionist view in most of mainland Britain (see Source 4). By mid-1987, the campaign against the Agreement had run out of steam.

SOURCE 2 A loyalist crowd demonstrating outside Belfast City Hall in November 1985. Estimates put the size of the crowd at about 100,000, comparable to the opposition to Home Rule in 1912–14 (see pages 38–40)

With hindsight, unionist fears were probably exaggerated. Although Garrett Fitzgerald hoped the Agreement would be a step to Irish unity, Mrs Thatcher's main aim was cross-border security to help tackle the IRA. There is some evidence that the Agreement did help to combat the IRA. However, its main effect was to give the SDLP a much-needed boost against Sinn Fein. In national and local elections in 1986–87, Sinn Fein support dropped significantly. Many nationalists could see that the way ahead was in moderation, and that the Agreement gave the Republic some say, however small, in Northern Ireland's affairs. Sinn Fein refused to accept the Agreement, and would not compromise in any way. Many Nationalists, therefore, were happy to return to the SDLP, who embraced the Agreement, now that there was a concrete achievement to be built on. They believed that the SDLP, through the Agreement, could call on the Republic's government to point out what they felt were injustices and abuses.

2. What does Source 2 tell historians about unionist opposition to the Anglo–Irish Agreement?
3. Look at Source 4. What is the cartoonist saying about the opponents of the Agreement?
4. In what ways do Sources 2 and 4 present different views of the opposition to the Agreement?

Continued violence

Despite the Agreement, the paramilitaries continued their campaign of violence, striking at a range of targets, as the timeline in Source 3 shows.

1987 An IRA bomb kills eleven people and injures over 60 at a Remembrance Day service in Enniskillen.
A single loyalist gunman kills three mourners at an IRA activist's funeral.

1988 Eight soldiers are killed by an IRA landmine.

1991 Loyalists kill 31 people in the course of the year, mostly innocent Catholics and usually as revenge for IRA attacks.

1992 The UFF kill five Catholic civilians in an attack on a betting shop.
A huge IRA bomb in central London causes up to £1 billion worth of damage.

1993 The IRA kill two young boys in Warrington with a bomb placed in a rubbish bin.
An IRA bomb goes off prematurely in a Shankill fish shop. The bomber and nine innocent Protestant civilians are killed.
Loyalist gunmen kill thirteen in revenge attacks for the Shankill bomb.

SOURCE 3 Selected examples of violence, 1987–93

SOURCE 4 A cartoon in the Belfast newspaper *Fortnight*, 8 January 1987. The three people in the boat, Margaret Thatcher, Neil Kinnock (Labour leader at the time) and David Steel (Liberal leader), are ignoring the protest. The two 'dinosaurs' are the Ulster Unionist leaders James Molyneaux and John Taylor. The 'dam' is Ian Paisley

THE DEFIANT DINOSAUR AT ITS DAM

Attempt 3: The Downing Street Declaration, 1993

- *This was agreed between Prime Minister John Major and the Taoiseach, Albert Reynolds.*
- *Talks were to be set up to decide on a new form of government for Northern Ireland.*
- *The new Northern Ireland government would respect all traditions in Northern Ireland.*
- *Only parties which rejected violence would be allowed any say in the talks.*
- *The British government said it had no selfish political or economic interest in Northern Ireland, but was concerned only with the welfare of all the people of Northern Ireland.*
- *The British government accepted that Irish unity was an issue for Irish people, but said that it could only happen with the consent of those in the North.*
- *The Irish government accepted the principle of consent for Irish unity.*
- *The Irish government also accepted that it might have to drop the parts of its constitution which claimed the North as part of its territory.*
- *The Irish government would set up a Forum for Peace and Reconciliation to promote trust and understanding between the traditions. Only those who rejected violence could be part of this.*

The late 1980s and early 1990s saw a horrific cycle of violence as Loyalists began to match Republicans in the number of killings they carried out (see page 105). However, some positive developments were also taking place at the same time.

There was also strong evidence that ordinary people in Northern Ireland were longing for peace more than ever. Sinn Fein lost the West Belfast seat to the SDLP in the general election of 1992, with Catholics and Protestants both voting SDLP. Thousands of people marched at peace rallies organised by the Irish Congress of Trade Unions after the Shankill bombing (see page 105). Much more activity was on a small scale and went largely unreported.

SOURCE 5 John Major and Albert Reynolds announce the Downing Street Declaration outside 10 Downing Street, 15 December 1993

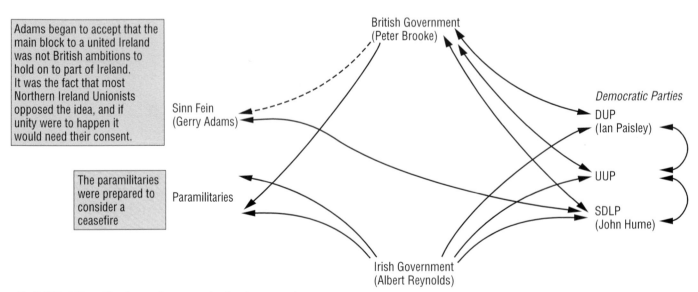

SOURCE 6 The lines of communication between the various groups in the conflict in the early 1990s

One person who did hit the headlines was the new Irish President, Mary Robinson, elected in 1990. She played a key role in changing attitudes towards nationalism in the Republic. She argued that peace and justice in Northern Ireland were more important than removing Partition. She also had a track record of sympathy for Unionists.

The end result of all the talking was the Downing Street Declaration of 15 December 1993. Prime Minister John Major stood outside 10 Downing Street with Taoiseach Albert Reynolds. In Northern Ireland, the Alliance Party and SDLP welcomed the Declaration. The Ulster Unionists cautiously accepted it. Mitchel McLaughlin of Sinn Fein saw it as very disappointing. Ian Paisley accused John Major of having 'sold out Ulster to buy off the fiendish republican scum'.

Despite this opposition, the Declaration had important results. The republican and loyalist paramilitaries studied it carefully and clarified details of the Declaration with the British government. (This allowed them to delay a formal acceptance of the Declaration without openly rejecting it.) However, they also continued to kill each other and innocent civilians at an appalling rate. In the summer of 1994, republican and loyalist paramilitaries engaged in a series of tit-for-tat killings, including the Loughinisland incident shown in Source 2 on page 90. Nevertheless, the politicians and some of the paramilitaries were now working towards an end to violence. In the next five years, Northern Ireland would come a long way.

■ ACTIVITY

You are a reporter in 1993. Most other reporters are writing articles about the Downing Street Declaration, which has just been signed. You have decided to be slightly different. You are going to look back at the political initiatives of the last twenty years in Northern Ireland, leading up to and including the Declaration. You could work alone or with a team of researchers to help you.

1. First copy and complete the chart below analysing the three initiatives.
2. Use your completed chart to write an article covering at least some of the following issues:

■ Have any policies or ideas come up several times in the political initiatives?
■ Have any policies been dropped?
■ How have the main political parties in Northern Ireland reacted to each of the initiatives?
■ Do any of the initiatives show one or more groups or parties compromising?
■ Have any initiatives successfully built on achievements of previous initiatives?

You should finish your report with a conclusion on whether you feel Northern Ireland is closer to peace in 1993, or whether it is no nearer than it was in 1973.

Initiative	Issues raised			Reactions to the initiative from ...			
	Self-government for Northern Ireland?	Cross-border organis-ations(s)?	Principle of consent?	Loyalists	Moderate Unionists	Moderate Nationalists	Republicans
1. The Power-Sharing Executive and the Sunningdale Agreement, 1973–74							
2. The Anglo–Irish Agreement, 1985							
3. The Downing Street Declaration, 1993							

■ REVIEW ACTIVITY – CHAPTERS 5 AND 6

The background

The year is 1994. As you have seen, Northern Ireland is experiencing a feeling of quiet but very, very cautious hope. The British government is looking at ways to set up a 'peace process'. However, the situation is very tense, and one false move or piece of bad publicity could ruin everything.

The situation

A conference is being held to discuss the way forward. The situation is so sensitive that the groups concerned are all meeting separately and communicating by fax, telephone and e-mail. You will belong to one of the following teams, and your job is to advise the government about your group's position in the Northern Ireland conflict:

1. Republican paramilitaries
2. Loyalist paramilitaries
3. Unionist politicians
4. Loyalist politicians
5. SDLP
6. Sinn Fein
7. Government of the Republic of Ireland
8. British government
9. The security forces.

The agenda

The agenda for the conference is very long, but you are only looking at the first two items:

1. 'Why has Northern Ireland's conflict proved impossible to resolve since 1969?'
2. 'Is the situation in 1994 better than it has been at any previous time?'

You will have to work in stages.

Stage 1

Take a long, hard look at your group's role in the conflict. You have to advise the government about:

- ways in which your group has helped promote peace
- ways in which it has caused conflict
- why and how your group thinks that its actions have been justified
- examples of actions taken by your group which it regrets, or feels the issue could have been dealt with differently.

Stage 2

When you have considered your group's actions, prepare a submission to the person chairing the whole conference. This submission must contain:

- a percentage mark, showing how responsible you feel your group is for the continuing conflict
- one or more actions which you feel your group could take in order to help the peace process to succeed (for example, changing your policies)
- actions which some of the other groups need to take (for example, declaring a ceasefire) which would make it easier for your group to fully support the peace process.

Stage 3

The chairperson of the conference will now give you the forms completed by the other groups in the conference. Look at the percentages and see if you agree with them. You must then decide:

whether you agree with the percentage figures (you can only do this if they add up to 100, but even then you might disagree)

or

whether you wish to come up with your own set of percentages for all nine groups.

Stage 4

Finally, your group must present its conclusions on the two agenda questions to the conference. This could be done as an oral presentation, or a written one, perhaps by e-mail. Remember to look back at the two questions you are being asked to tackle.

■ COURSEWORK ASSIGNMENT

'Was the situation in Northern Ireland in 1994 better than it had been at any previous time?'

Your answer to this question should refer to at least some of the following issues:

- Why were the actions or attitudes of paramilitary groups changing by 1994?
- How much were they changing?

- How had political initiatives helped to improve the situation in Northern Ireland (for example, through improved security and/or tackling difficult political problems)?
- How had the actions of individual politicians and ordinary people helped to improve the situation?

You will also need to include the following:

- arguments to support the view that the situation in Northern Ireland was not improving
- your own conclusions.

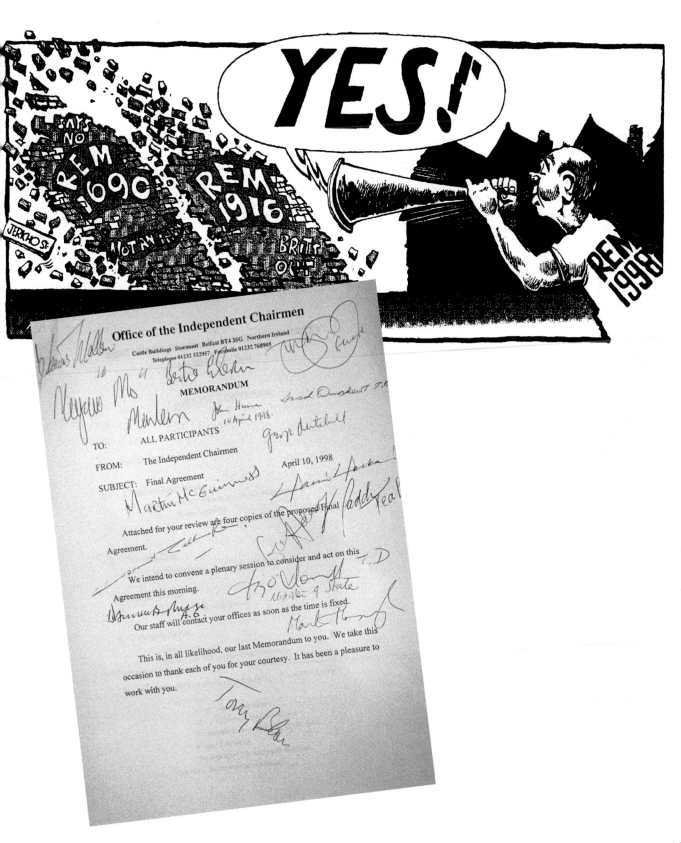

Fast track: Five steps to the Good Friday Agreement of 1998

THE 1993 DOWNING Street Declaration did not bring peace. The years 1993–98 were to see a long and difficult 'peace process'.

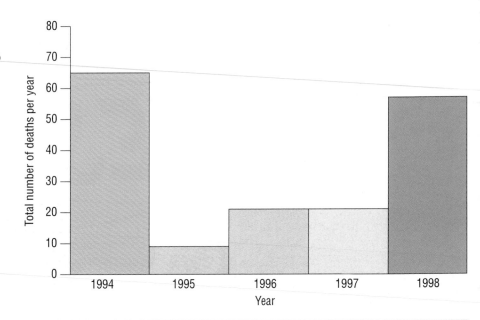

SOURCE 1 Deaths in the Troubles

■ TASK A

Many of the politicians involved in the peace process of 1993–98 described it as a rollercoaster ride of high points and low points. Your aim in this activity is to decide what you think the high and low points were.

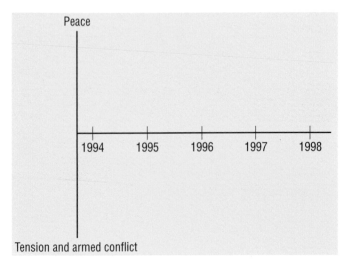

1. Make your own copy of this diagram and follow these instructions to complete it.
2. Read through the outline of events of 1993–98 on pages 111–115.
3. As you read, select events which you think are particularly important. Some examples are given below but you can add more events if you can think of them.
4. Put each selected event somewhere on the graph. First of all, make sure you have it in the right year. Secondly, decide whether you feel this event made a major contribution to peace or seriously got in the way of peace.
5. Finally, narrow down your choices to six events or developments:
   a) four which made the most important contributions to achieving peace
   b) two which represent the lowest points in the process when peace seemed furthest away.

Suggested events
- IRA ceasefire
- Loyalist ceasefire
- Joint Framework Document
- Lowest death toll
- Trimble commits his party to the peace process
- Clinton's visit to Northern Ireland
- Orange Order calls off marches
- Clinton keeps the parties talking
- Negotiations at Stormont
- Good Friday Agreement
- Referendum
- Republicans request clarification of Downing Street Declaration
- Highest death toll
- IRA refuses to decommission weapons
- Arguments over elections
- IRA bombs in London
- Violence at Drumcree
- Republican divisions
- Unionist divisions

1994: Paramilitary ceasefires

After the apparent advances in 1993, 1994 did not start well. In January, the Republicans asked for clarification of the Downing Street Declaration: they clearly did not like it. There was more tension later that month when the US President Bill Clinton gave Sinn Fein leader Gerry Adams a visa, allowing him to meet with Irish–American groups in the USA. This turned out to be an important decision. Irish Americans confirmed the views put forward to Sinn Fein by John Hume in his talks with Adams. Some new thinking was now beginning to emerge within the republican movement (see Source 2). This became clear on 31 August when the IRA announced a complete ceasefire. On 13 October, the loyalist paramilitaries also declared a ceasefire. There were no wild celebrations – people had seen many ceasefires come and go. Nevertheless, Christmas 1994 was the most peaceful for many years in Northern Ireland.

■ TASK B

1. Write a summary of the new approach to republican policy being set out in Source 2.
2. Do you think a nationalist politician like John Hume would have felt satisfied on reading Source 2?
3. If you had been one of the politicians in Northern Ireland in 1994, would you have been encouraged by Source 3? Explain your answer.

SOURCE 2 An extract from the secret Totally Unarmed Strategy (TUAS) document circulated within the IRA in June–July 1994. The document was drawn up as a result of talks between John Hume and Gerry Adams and Adams' talks with Irish Americans

66 *After prolonged discussion, the leadership decided that it would be prepared to use the TUAS option. It would have to get agreement with the Dublin government, the SDLP and the Irish–American lobby to advance basic republican principles. The leadership believes there is enough in common to create a substantial political momentum, which will considerably advance the struggle at this time. The leadership has now decided that there is enough agreement to proceed with the TUAS option.* 99

SOURCE 3 David Ervine, leader of the Progressive Unionist Party, speaking in 1994, soon after the loyalist ceasefire. The PUP represented the loyalist paramilitary group the Ulster Volunteer Force (UVF)

66 *We are all guilty in this society to one degree or another; whether it be by word or deed or silence. And frankly we all have to acknowledge to some degree our guilt in order to clear the playing surface so that we can move forward. The loyalist paramilitaries have said for 25 years that their violence was reactive to IRA violence. The IRA's violence has ceased. Therefore, the Loyalists, given that their constitutional position is safe as a partner within the United Kingdom, have also stopped.* 99

SOURCE 4 An enthusiastic reception for the *Belfast Telegraph* declaring news of the IRA ceasefire, 31 August 1994

1995: The Joint Framework Document

The ceasefires were followed by the Joint Framework Document published in February 1995. This agreement was drawn up by the British and Irish governments and set out a plan for a peace process in Northern Ireland, including a new assembly for Northern Ireland and a North–South Council of Ministers with influence over a range of issues. It set the 'agenda' for the talks which resulted in the Good Friday Agreement. It was generally welcomed, and 1995 saw Northern Ireland's lowest death toll in the Troubles.

However, there were still problems:

■ Unionists were suspicious about the plan for a North–South Council of Ministers: would it lead to a united Ireland?
■ Unionists and the British government wanted to see DECOMMISSIONING of IRA weapons, but Sinn Fein said the IRA would not give up weapons because it did not trust the British government.

■ Many members of paramilitary groups were in prison: would they now be released early, and how would the families of the victims feel about this?

Despite these major difficulties, peace now looked possible. In September, the new Ulster Unionist Party leader, David Trimble, confirmed his full support for the peace process. In October, an international commission under former US Senator George Mitchell was set up to work out a process for decommissioning weapons and achieving a settlement which everyone could accept. Mitchell had enormous experience as a negotiator and peacemaker. The respected journalist and writer on Northern Ireland Peter Taylor believes that 'without Mitchell's patience and personal, political and diplomatic skills, it is unlikely that the Good Friday Agreement would ever have been finalised'.

1. The year 1995 saw many positive developments in the peace process. What would you say were the two most important? Explain your answer.

SOURCE 5 Senator George Mitchell (centre) with SDLP leader John Hume (left) and Sinn Fein leader Gerry Adams

1996: Decommissioning and elections

The following year, 1996, was another dramatic period in the peace process. In January, Senator Mitchell set out the 'Mitchell Principles', a plan for achieving decommissioning of paramilitary weapons. Sinn Fein agreed to the Principles, but the IRA leadership said it did not, and refused to hand over any arms.

As a result, the British government demanded elections in Northern Ireland: Prime Minister John Major wanted to see how much support the paramilitaries had. Nationalists were outraged, because new elections meant delays in the peace process.

In February, tension turned to despair as the IRA detonated a huge bomb in London's Docklands, followed by another in Manchester in June. In July, violence erupted at Drumcree, near Portadown, as Catholic residents objected to an Orange Order march through their neighbourhood. On the positive side, the loyalist ceasefire held, and in June the elections to the Northern Ireland Forum took place without violent incidents in Northern Ireland.

The Forum was a new body. Its full title was the Northern Ireland Forum for Political Dialogue. Its job was to consider and examine issues relevant to promoting dialogue and understanding within Northern Ireland. Essentially it was a sounding board body to work out all the issues which would have to be tackled in the peace process.

2. List the positive and negative developments in 1996. Would you say that the positive developments outweighed the negative ones or not? Explain your answer.

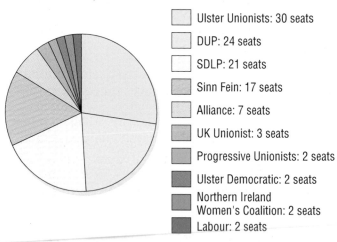

- Ulster Unionists: 30 seats
- DUP: 24 seats
- SDLP: 21 seats
- Sinn Fein: 17 seats
- Alliance: 7 seats
- UK Unionist: 3 seats
- Progressive Unionists: 2 seats
- Ulster Democratic: 2 seats
- Northern Ireland Women's Coalition: 2 seats
- Labour: 2 seats

SOURCE 6 Results of the Northern Ireland Forum elections, June 1996

SOURCE 7 Ulster Unionist Party leader David Trimble surveys the British Army barricades preventing Orange Lodge marchers from walking down the Garvaghy Road from Drumcree church to Portadown

1997: New governments and deep divisions

May 1997 saw a new Prime Minister, Tony Blair, elected in the UK, and in June there was a new Irish Taoiseach, Bertie Aherne. Blair appointed Dr Mo Mowlam as Northern Ireland Secretary. She was to play an important role in the peace process, and both nationalist and unionist politicians admired her abilities as a negotiator. She organised many events at Stormont and encouraged people (from the nationalist community in particular) not to associate Stormont with their bitter memories of the past.

Dr Mowlam was soon fully aware of just how tough her new job was. There was more IRA violence in June, and for the second year running clashes occurred between police and Loyalists over the Drumcree march in July. In a much-praised move, the Orange Order voluntarily called off other potentially controversial parades to help ease the tension.

In July, the IRA announced a new ceasefire. This allowed Sinn Fein to take part in the peace process negotiations, but it did not lead to the decommissioning of any weapons. Unionists were divided over whether or not they should sit down to talks with Sinn Fein while the IRA still had all its weapons. The DUP pulled out of the peace process in September, but David Trimble did not. He remained committed to it, despite bitter criticism from some fellow Unionists and despite the fact that he himself was unhappy with some aspects of the process.

The Republicans were also divided. In November, some members of the IRA left the movement because they did not support Sinn Fein's participation in the peace process. They set up their own republican splinter groups, Continuity IRA and the Real IRA.

1998: The Good Friday Agreement

- *A new Northern Ireland Assembly with 108 members would be set up. All key decisions would require the consent of both communities in the province.*
- *A North–South Council of Ministers would also be set up, made up of members of the new Assembly and ministers from the Republic.*
- *The Irish government would remove Articles 2 and 3 of its constitution, which claimed the North as part of its territory (subject to a referendum of the people of the Republic).*
- *There would be a review of policing in Northern Ireland.*
- *Early release for paramilitary prisoners was promised.*

SOURCE 8 A cartoon from the *Guardian*, January 1998, referring to Mo Mowlam's visit to the Maze prison. One of the prisoners she spoke to was called John 'Mad Dog' Adair

SOURCE 9 Former IRA activist Gabriel Megahy, interviewed on BBC television in 1998

66 *I'm prepared as a Republican to settle. My hopes are for the unification of this country, but I have to accept in the long run that it's not going to happen. The Brits are not going to sail away in the sunlight. Go back to war? What are we going to do? It would only cause more misery, more suffering and mostly to our own people and to ourselves.* 99

The early part of 1998 saw some extraordinary events. There was a crisis in January, when it seemed likely that loyalist paramilitary prisoners would withdraw their support for the peace process. This would be a major blow, as they had immense influence within their movement. Both the Ulster Unionist leader David Trimble and the Northern Ireland Secretary Mo Mowlam visited them in the Maze prison and regained their support. It was now becoming clear that most loyalist and republican paramilitaries were prepared to end the conflict. However, some paramilitary groups were still prepared to fight. In February and March, a series of bombings and shootings occurred. These were carried out by loyalist and republican splinter groups who had rejected the peace process.

The parties taking part in the talks had agreed a deadline of 9 April to reach an agreement. As the deadline approached, the negotiations gathered pace. President Clinton worked behind the scenes, encouraging various leaders to talk or to compromise. From 6 April onwards, Tony Blair, Bertie Aherne and the Northern Ireland leaders were negotiating non-stop at Stormont.

SOURCE 10 Senator George Mitchell commenting on the contribution of Taoiseach Bertie Aherne and British Prime Minister Tony Blair in the talks leading up to the Good Friday Agreement. Mitchell was the head of the commission which set up and ran the talks

66 *I had not personally seen a finer example of leadership in a democratic society than that exhibited by Tony Blair and Bertie Aherne in these talks ... When Bertie Aherne and Tony Blair came here there was no agreement. They worked. They didn't supervise the negotiations, they conducted the negotiations, word by word, sentence by sentence, provision by provision. There would not have been an agreement without them. They were superb.* 99

SOURCE 11 A cartoon by Martyn Turner, published in the *Irish Times* on 25 May 1998. 'Rem' stands for 'Remember'

On the afternoon of Saturday 10 April, the talks chairman, Senator Mitchell, made a statement:

'I am pleased to announce that the two governments and the political parties of Northern Ireland have reached an agreement.'

However, the Agreement was only the beginning. The crunch was to come in a REFERENDUM to be held in May 1998. The people of the Republic and of Northern Ireland were asked whether they accepted the Good Friday Agreement. The people of the Republic were also asked whether they were prepared to allow Articles 2 and 3 of their constitution (claiming the North as part of the Republic) to be removed. The result in the Republic was overwhelmingly in favour – 94 per cent. In Northern Ireland, the majority was smaller, but it was a clear majority of 71 per cent. It was a moment of history, but was it just the achievement of the politicians? That is what most of the rest of this chapter is about.

3. Look carefully at the terms of the Good Friday Agreement on page 114. Which terms would be regarded as sensitive or controversial
   a) in Northern Ireland
   b) in the Republic
   c) in mainland Britain?
4. Source 8 is meant to be humorous, but also attempts to get across an important point. What point is the cartoonist trying to make about Mo Mowlam?
5. Source 9 quotes a republican activist who is prepared to give up some important aims in order to gain peace. What evidence is there in this section of other groups making important compromises as well?

■ **ACTIVITY**

When this book was being prepared, there was a lot of discussion about Source 11. Some people thought that it should go in Chapter 2. Others thought that it should go on the front cover. The author thought that Source 11 belonged here. Prepare a short letter or e-mail to the author explaining:

■ whether you think the source is or is not in the right place, and why
■ why you think the other suggested places were or were not right for it.

SOURCE 1 A cartoon from the *London Evening Standard*, 29 October 1982

MANY COMMENTATORS OUTSIDE Northern Ireland have tended to see the 1998 Agreement as the achievement of the politicians. However, the politicians could not have reached the Agreement if ordinary people did not want and work for peace. And did they want peace? Of course! For three decades, the continual media coverage of the Troubles gave the impression that everyone in Northern Ireland was an extremist involved in the conflict on one side or the other. However, Source 2 is closer to the truth. It was drawn by someone living in Belfast at the time. As you can see, it looks at the relationship between the men of violence and the ordinary people in a very different way.

1. Sources 1 and 2 are both similar and different in terms of what they say about the Irish people. Explain these similarities and differences.

Normal life

If you remember nothing else about this chapter, remember this: throughout the Troubles, *most people in Northern Ireland lived normal lives for most of the time.* That was what they wanted. Even when they were affected by the Troubles, most people did not nurse a grievance, or become extremists. Most simply wanted to get back to normal life as quickly as possible. Even in politics, there was a strong focus on the everyday issues of normal life.

SOURCE 2 A cartoon by Martyn Turner published in the *Irish Times* in 1993

SOURCE 3 Extracts from a speech by a senior BBC journalist in Northern Ireland, Richard Francis

❝ *In Northern Ireland, our extensive coverage of sport, our sponsorship of musicians, writers and actors, the daily advertising of events and discussion of household matters in regional programmes such as* Good Morning Ulster *[and]* Taste of Hunni, *and our access and community programmes, are all about normal life. More than 80 per cent of Radio Ulster's output is concerned with normality.* ❞

Peace movements

Northern Ireland's people did not just keep their heads down during the Troubles. One way in which they opposed violence was to vote for the political parties that opposed violence. Another way was to take part in some of the many peace movements and community groups in the Province. Here are just a few examples.

The 1970s: The Peace People

On 10 August 1976, Betty Williams watched in horror as an IRA getaway car being chased by soldiers ploughed into Anne Maguire and her children: three children were killed. Betty Williams and Anne Maguire's sister, Mairead Corrigan, felt they had to do something. With the help and guidance of the journalist Ciaran McKeown they launched the Peace People.

During the rest of 1976, Belfast and the rest of Northern Ireland witnessed huge rallies calling for peace, organised by the Peace People. Some 20,000 people turned up for a rally in Belfast's Ormeau Park on 21 August. A week later, the same number marched through the loyalist heartland of the Shankill Road. About 25,000 gathered in Londonderry in early September. The numbers were impressive, but not as impressive as the sight of Shankill residents walking and talking with Catholic priests and nuns.

Money and support poured in, especially from abroad. The Peace People tried to do practical things with the money, setting up community projects and giving grants and loans. The crowning moment for the movement came in 1977, when Betty Williams and Mairead Corrigan were awarded the Nobel Peace Prize.

However, by the end of the 1970s the movement was beginning to experience problems. Some other peace groups and community workers felt that they were being marginalised by the Peace People. There were disputes over the movement's funds. Some sections of the press were hostile to the Peace People. According to the leading Irish historian J.J. Lee, politicians and paramilitaries saw the Peace People as a threat to their own interests. They began to circulate rumours or simply attack them directly. For example, Paisley's DUP described the movement as counterproductive and UDA publications attacked them as tools of the Republicans, while Sinn Fein publications regularly attacked them as agents of the British.

The fatal blow came when the leading figures in the movement disagreed. The Peace People collapsed in 1980. They had not been able to bridge the divisions in Northern Ireland society.

SOURCE 4 A Peace People poster from 1976, showing Betty Williams

SOURCE 5 An extract from *The Politics of Irish Freedom*, written by Sinn Fein leader Gerry Adams in 1986 and updated in 1994

66 *The Peace People lost credibility in nationalist areas very quickly. In fact, what credibility it had had consisted basically of sympathy for the Maguires ... It was an attempt to move people away from republican physical force politics, and it failed because it did not seek to remedy the reasons why people felt compelled to have recourse to physical force. As soon as they tried to examine what peace was and how it could be attained, the leadership of the Peace People began to collapse ...* 99

2. Read Source 5 carefully.
a) Write a brief summary of Adams's explanation for the failure of the Peace People.
b) Would Professor J.J. Lee (see text opposite) regard Source 5 as a trustworthy explanation of the collapse of the Peace People? Explain your answer.

117

The 1980s: Gordon Wilson

Gordon Wilson came from the unionist community in Enniskillen. In November 1987, he was at the Enniskillen Remembrance Day ceremony with his daughter, who was killed when an IRA bomb went off. Many people in Northern Ireland have experienced devastating losses, but Wilson's reaction set him apart. He went on to devote his life to working for peace and reconciliation between the communities in Northern Ireland. He played an important role in numerous peace groups. In 1993, he was made a Senator of the Republic of Ireland. He advised the politicians and civil servants who put together the Joint Framework Document (see page 112). Above all, he was critical of anyone who refused to compromise.

SOURCE 6   Gordon Wilson's reaction to the death of his daughter

66 *I bear no ill will. I bear no grudge. Dirty talk of that sort will not bring her back to life. She was a great wee lassie. She loved her profession. She was a pet. She's dead. She's in Heaven and we'll meet again. Don't ask me, please, for a purpose ... I don't have an answer ... It's part of a greater plan, and God is good, and we shall meet again.* 99

SOURCE 7   Part of a speech by Gordon Wilson in March 1995

66 *1690 was over three centuries ago: we are heading for the 21st century. Time has moved on. I appeal above all to politicians to stop playing politics with people's lives, to look over their shoulder and to listen to what their grassroots supporters are saying ... They said that they want their political leaders to talk ... It seems to me that the man and woman in the street are prepared to compromise. Compromise is not giving in, it is maturity. I appeal to the political leaders to sit down, all of them, to listen to their electors, to present their policies, to reach out to love their neighbours and their common God, and so to help us towards achieving peace.* 99

3. Northern Ireland is part of the UK, while the Republic is not. Gordon Wilson's death in 1995 was commemorated by a minute's silence in the Irish Dail. He was much less well known in the UK. What does this suggest about British attitudes to Northern Ireland?

Community groups

Gordon Wilson was certainly not unique in wanting peace and reconciliation. Throughout the Troubles, many local community groups have helped victims, or have tried to improve relations between the communities. Here are just a few.

Ballynafeigh Community Development Association

This group was formed in the 1970s to try to preserve the mixed nature of housing in its locality. It provides welfare advice, after-school activities, crèche facilities and a host of other services to improve the lives of local people. Find out more about them on the internet by doing a search of their name.

The Ulster Project Northern Ireland

This was founded in the mid-1970s to develop cross-community communication. The Project organises trips to fourteen areas of the USA for mixed groups of fourteen- to fifteen-year-olds. Away from Northern Ireland, they begin to learn about communities other than their own, and usually find out how similar they are. By the 1990s, around 4000 students had taken part, and not one had become involved in paramilitary activity. Find out more by searching on the internet.

The Peace Train

The Peace Train was set up in 1989 to highlight paramilitary attacks on the Dublin to Belfast railway and the damage this did both to relations between the Republic and Northern Ireland and also to the economy. It ran special trains with low fares to encourage people to travel to and fro between the two capitals.

SOURCE 8 *Enough is Enough!* A leaflet advertising a peace rally organised by Belfast trade unions, 1998

SOURCE 9 A peace rally in Belfast involving trade unions and other groups who want peace

Trade unions

The trade union movement was a powerful force in bringing people together to work for peace, especially in the 1990s. The huge attendance of both Protestants and Catholics at rallies like the one in Source 9 made clear to the politicians and paramilitaries the feelings of ordinary people in Northern Ireland.

Education and the Churches

Another important way in which people showed their desire to end conflict was through education. The Department of Education for Northern Ireland (DENI) set up its EMU (Education for Mutual Understanding) programme in the 1980s. This was a set of broad principles designed to be integrated into lessons. Thus, a history teacher might look at a balanced view of Irish history or an English teacher might base lessons around respecting the values of others. Progress was slow but steady, and many schools and colleges had well-developed EMU policies by the 1990s.

These programmes were helped by the majority of Northern Ireland's Churches. In 1978, the Irish Council of Churches established the Churches' Peace Education Programme. This programme produced resources for schools, and worked with DENI to promote EMU.

SOURCE 10 Lagan College was founded in 1981 as an INTEGRATED school, educating Catholics and Protestants together. The aim of the school was that students from different backgrounds should get to know each other

■ TASK

Look back at pages 116–119. Write a list of six short points for an internet fact sheet on the Northern Ireland Troubles. Your title is 'Six things about Northern Ireland which you never see on the TV news'. Concentrate on efforts to bring about peace and reconciliation.

How did people in the Republic and in Britain help?

People in Britain and the Irish Republic played an important role in creating the right conditions for the Agreement in 1998. One of the key developments in the Republic was a new feeling among the great majority that Partition no longer mattered. This was partly a result of rapid social and political changes in the late 1980s and early 1990s. The influence of the Catholic Church seemed to be weakening, and the Republic's economy began to boom, with the help of investment from the European Union. People in the Republic saw the question of Northern Ireland as only one political issue, and not the most important by any means.

During the Troubles, it was often said that people in the Republic took too much interest in the affairs of Northern Ireland. This was certainly not true of people in Britain. However, in the 1990s, the popularity of Irish culture in Britain created greater public interest in Ireland. Organisations such as the Warrington Project have been working to increase young people's understanding of the Irish situation (see Source 13). This project was set up after the Warrington bomb of 1993, which killed two young boys from the town. It organises links between schoolchildren in Britain, the Republic and Northern Ireland, and carries out educational projects. (You can learn more about the Warrington Project from its website at http://www.warrington.gov.uk/wp/home.htm) Students in Britain also began to study the Troubles in history lessons, through the Modern World Study of the Schools History Project.

These developments gave politicians the incentive and support they needed to invest time and effort into attempts to reach a solution.

SOURCE 11 The cartoonist Martyn Turner writing about attitudes in the Republic in 1995

66 *The Provisionals' [IRA] campaign of the last 25 years has brought about a sea change of attitudes in the Irish Republic. It is no coincidence, for example, that the flagship papers of Irish nationalism, the Irish Press Group, have just gone down the swannee, whilst the most virulent anti-Provo organ in the state, the* Sunday Independent, *goes from strength to strength. Down here we watch as much, if not more, British television as our own. We read more foreign (British) newspapers than any other country in the world. We celebrate Ireland through U2 and the Cranberries and a soccer team made up of Englishmen, and make pronouncements about the Famine guaranteed not to cause offence to our European neighbours. This isn't the country of Ian Paisley's nightmares any more. It's a place where the price of Irish unity is discussed before the necessity of it.* 99

SOURCE 12 A Martyn Turner cartoon from 1995

TEENAGERS DON'T WANT WALLS OF

HATE
FEAR
DEATH
LIES
HURT
PAIN
GUNS

THE WARRINGTON PROJECT

Promoting mutual understanding between the peoples of Britain and the island of Ireland at community level

SOURCE 13 The work of the Warrington Project. The Project publishes free material for schools in Britain. The materials all contain an Irish dimension and are mainly for History and English lessons. The aim is to help young British people learn more about Ireland and understand its problems more clearly

■ COURSEWORK ASSIGNMENT: THE ROLE OF ORDINARY PEOPLE

On page 126 at the end of this chapter there is a suggested Coursework Assignment. It asks you to analyse the factors which made the Good Friday Agreement of 1998 possible. If you have found studying ordinary people (as opposed to politicians or paramilitaries) interesting, why not ask your teacher whether you can focus your assignment on ordinary people? A possible title might be:

'The single most important factor in promoting peace in Northern Ireland throughout the Troubles has been the attitude of ordinary people.' Do you agree with this statement?

Your coursework will have to answer at least some of these questions:

1. Did ordinary people want peace?
2. How much did ordinary people support the paramilitaries?
3. How important were political initiatives?
4. Would political initiatives have worked without ordinary people?

Doing this assignment will involve research using different sections of this book and other resources as well.

■ TASK

Look closely at Source 1 on page 116. For many people in England this cartoon summed up the violence of Northern Ireland and the Irish in a nutshell. The cartoon caused outrage when it was published. Most Irish people and their descendants living in England felt it was an insult. Many Irish-owned businesses refused to advertise in the *Evening Standard*. So did Ken Livingstone, then the Leader of the Greater London Council.

Your job is to analyse carefully all of the things the cartoon is saying about Irish people. Then, write a letter to the *Standard* complaining about the cartoon. You must take each of the points made in the cartoon and, using all you have found out over pages 116–121, explain why you feel this is not a fair representation of ordinary Irish people. Your teacher will give you a photocopy of the cartoon to make notes on.

Has international interest in Northern Ireland helped or hindered peace?

International revolution

The conflict in Northern Ireland has always had an international dimension. The IRA saw themselves as part of a worldwide movement of fighters for freedom. Murals in republican areas draw links between the IRA's campaign and revolutionary movements in West Africa and South America. The IRA believed their campaign was particularly similar to the struggle of the Palestinian Liberation Organisation (PLO) against Israel in the Middle East. This may have helped the IRA to gain and keep support in some countries. For example, the Libyan leader Colonel Gadaffi supported the IRA because he saw them as a revolutionary movement with similar ideas and aims to his own. Gadaffi often clashed with Britain and the USA over their policies in the Middle East, which helps to explain his support for the IRA.

SOURCE 1 A mural from the Falls Road. It links the IRA with the PLO and the South West African People's Organisation in Namibia. It emphasises in particular the links between the women of these movements, showing a member of Cumann na mBann (the IRA women's movement)

SOURCE 2 The front page of *An Phoblacht*, 10 June 1982. (Israeli forces invaded the Lebanon in 1982 to try to destroy PLO forces which had bases there)

However, this international dimension damaged support for the IRA in other countries. Many regarded Gadaffi as a terrorist and Libya as a terrorist state. US President Ronald Reagan actually bombed Libya in 1986 in retaliation for alleged terrorist actions by the Libyan government. The PLO were seen as terrorists rather than freedom fighters in most western countries. This was especially true in the USA, which has a large and influential Jewish population whose sympathies lay with the state of Israel, not with the PLO.

■ TASK

Why did Republicans emphasise that they were part of an international revolution?
In groups discuss the following questions:

1. How would this make their actions seem more acceptable?
2. How would this generate support – for example in training, finance and weapons?
3. How would it affect members of their own movement?

Irish America and republicanism

The really important international connection is with the USA (as well as with Britain, of course). In the eighteenth century many Presbyterians left Ulster for a new life in the American colonies. They were to play a major role in the American Revolution and the establishment of the USA. In the mid-nineteenth century, the stream of emigrants became a flood. Ireland's rising population was devastated by famine in the 1840s. About a million people died and another 1.5 million emigrated to the USA.

Emigration continued after the famine, and many Irish communities prospered in American cities. They remembered the famine, and supported the Fenians against British rule (see page 43). They also supported the constitutional nationalism of Parnell later in the nineteenth century. This anti-British attitude continued into the twentieth century, although it varied in strength at different times.

British policy in Ireland was one of the few sources of tension between the British and US governments. Having said that, when a major issue emerged, Irish affairs were quickly ignored. At the end of the First World War, the claims of Sinn Fein to a place at the peace talks were ignored. During the Second World War, the need to defeat Germany outweighed any possible disputes between Britain and the USA about Ireland.

Irish America and the Troubles

When the Troubles broke out in 1969, many Irish Americans became interested and involved in Irish affairs. They were generally pro-Nationalist. However, while events such as Bloody Sunday created support for republicanism, IRA violence could destroy this support just as quickly. As a result, the republican movement in the USA consisted of a core of dedicated hardliners, and was never a mass movement.

Some of these hardliners helped to supply the IRA with weapons. The American Armalite rifle became part of republican folklore when IRA activists first acquired it. It was powerful, accurate and could be dismantled, which made it the perfect weapon for the campaigns the IRA was waging. Estimates varied, but US officials believed that around 50 per cent of IRA weapons in the 1970s came from the USA. British and Irish estimates put the figure at nearer 80 per cent. Organisations such as the Irish Northern Aid Committee (better known as Noraid) raised money for victims of the Troubles, but it was generally believed that most of the money went to support the IRA.

1. Explain how Sources 3 and 4 show different sides of Irish–American attitudes to Northern Ireland.
2. Is Source 5 evidence that IRA gun running was successful or unsuccessful? Explain your answer.

SOURCE 3 The reaction of US Senator Edward Kennedy to the Widgery Report into Bloody Sunday, 1972. Kennedy was a leading Irish American, and his views were widely shared in the USA

66 *Just as the injustice of internment was compounded by the torture of the men imprisoned, so the slaughter at Londonderry is being compounded by the arbitrary limits of the scope of the inquiry being held by Lord Widgery. Just as Ulster is Britain's Vietnam, so Bloody Sunday is Britain's My Lai [a massacre of civilians by US troops during the Vietnam war].* 99

SOURCE 4 The reaction of the *Chicago Tribune* to an IRA bomb in Hyde Park in 1982. There was a similar reaction in most US newspapers, and this condemnation continued in reaction to other IRA attacks during the 1980s

66 *IRA front groups ... claim that they are raising funds for the families of slain or imprisoned IRA men. They lie. The money goes for arms, ammunition and bombs. It buys the high explosives and the remote-control detonators that blew up in London. The money bankrolls the sort of sub-humans who can pack six-inch nails around a bomb and put it in a place where women and children and tourists will gather.* 99

SOURCE 5 Arms captured aboard the trawler the *Marita Ann*. It was seized in 1984, after a long investigation and undercover operation by the American authorities. Several IRA activists and a huge arsenal of weapons were on board when it was captured. The American investigation into the *Marita Ann* threw up links between gun running, organised crime in the USA and the illegal drugs trade. The huge size of the haul indicated how much more weaponry was probably getting through

Irish America and the peace process

In the 1990s, Irish America played a key role in the peace process. The SDLP leader John Hume had many contacts with Irish Americans. He and the Irish diplomat Michael Lillis convinced leading Irish Americans to take a stand supporting Irish unity but rejecting violent methods. One of those Hume convinced was Senator Edward Kennedy, brother of the assassinated President J.F. Kennedy and a very influential figure in the Irish–American business community. This Irish–American lobby kept the spotlight on Northern Ireland and convinced several US presidents to take an interest.

When Bill Clinton became President in 1993, he was already interested in Northern Ireland (as well as being keen to get the Irish–American vote on his side). In January 1994, he took the risky decision to give Sinn Fein leader Gerry Adams a visa to visit the USA, despite opposition from Britain. As Source 6 shows, the risk seemed to pay off.

3. In 1998, President Clinton was asked about the decision to give Adams a visa to enter the USA. He said, 'It was a judgement call. You asked me whether I think I did the right thing? I do.'
a) Explain why the decision was so risky.
b) Do you agree with Clinton's opinion? Explain your answer.

Clinton also communicated with the Unionists. In April 1994, he welcomed UUP and DUP delegations to Washington. The loyalist parties with paramilitary links also spoke to US government officials in October 1994. The US public's understanding of the Northern Ireland conflict was broadened by a live debate between Gerry Adams and Ulster Unionist Ken Maginnis on national television. Clinton and the Irish–American business community made it clear that if peace could be achieved there would be massive investment in Northern Ireland from the USA. It was one more incentive to achieve a settlement.

SOURCE 6 An extract from *The Fight for Peace*, by Eamonn Mallie and David McKittrick, published in 1997. Both authors are journalists for UK newspapers

66 *It now seems that Adams's treatment as an international statesman in New York reinforced his position within the republican movement and helped generate greater momentum for peace. President Clinton had made a very difficult decision in granting the visa. He opposed his own government agencies and antagonised the British. He also ran the risk of the IRA greatly embarrassing him by committing a major act of violence. Many leading Irish–American politicians and business people had similarly gone out on a limb for Adams. This put considerable pressure on the Sinn Fein president to reward the confidence shown in him, by helping to deliver an end to IRA violence. Adams later acknowledged that, 'By granting me a visa to come to the US, Mr Clinton helped create the conditions for the ceasefire.'* 99

SOURCE 7 President Clinton being introduced to a Belfast audience by two children from local Catholic and Protestant schools, November 1995. Clinton visited Northern Ireland in November 1995 and September 1998. He also visited the Republic of Ireland. He gave consistent support to Unionists and Nationalists trying to achieve peace

The European dimension

The European Union (EU) helped in the progress towards peace in a variety of ways. It contributed directly by putting some £400 million into a wide variety of projects in Northern Ireland and the Republic. Much of the money went on schemes which aimed to improve community relations or partnerships. Several projects brought representatives of Sinn Fein and the DUP together for the first time.

SOURCE 8 In 1998 SDLP leader John Hume and Ulster Unionist leader David Trimble were jointly awarded the Nobel Peace Prize. This is an extract from John Hume's speech at the ceremony

66 *In my own work for peace, I was very strongly inspired by my European experience. On my first visit to Strasbourg in 1979, as a member of the European Parliament, I went for a walk across the bridge from Strasbourg to Kohl. Strasbourg is in France, Kohl is in Germany. They are very close. I stopped in the middle of the bridge and I meditated. There is Germany. There is France. If I had stood on this bridge 30 years ago, after the end of the Second World War, when 25 million people lay dead across our continent for the second time in this century, and if I had said: 'Don't worry. In 30 years' time we will all be together in a new Europe, our conflicts and wars will be ended and we will be working together in our common interests,' I would have been sent to a psychiatrist. But it has happened and it is now clear that European Union is the best example in the history of the world of conflict resolution, and it is the duty of everyone, particularly those who live in areas of conflict, to study how it was done and to apply its principles to their own conflict resolution.* 99

SOURCE 9 Refugees fleeing the civil war in the former Yugoslavia. 1.3 million people became homeless refugees during the war. More people were killed in three years than throughout the 30 years of the Troubles in Northern Ireland

The EU was also important in shaping attitudes in the Republic. The Republic prospered in the 1990s, and its booming economy owed a great deal to the EU. As a result, many people saw themselves as Irish Europeans. As borders between traditionally hostile states began to become irrelevant all over Europe, many people started to feel the same about the North–South border in Ireland.

Civil wars

As the peace process in the 1990s faced its various challenges, television news brought pictures to Northern Ireland of civil war in Bosnia, Somalia and Rwanda. The unimaginable bloodshed and horror of those places reminded people in Northern Ireland of what could happen if paramilitaries rather than politicians were in control. It was a small factor, but a significant one in many people's minds.

4. Describe how the EU's work contributed to peace in Northern Ireland.
5. How does this contribution compare with that of the USA?
6. How do you think the Bosnian conflict affected the attitude of
a) paramilitary leaders
b) paramilitary 'troops'
c) ordinary people?

■ TASK

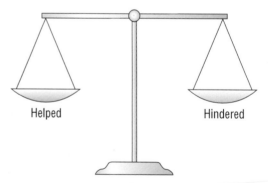

Draw your own version of this diagram. Use pages 122–125 to decide in what ways the international connection has helped bring peace in Northern Ireland, and in what ways it has hindered it. You could consider

■ the activities of Irish Americans
■ the IRA's connections with Libya and the PLO
■ the actions of the European Union
■ events such as the civil war in Bosnia.

Write each factor on one or other side of the scales.

■ REVIEW TASK

1. Use the information and sources on pages 110–125 to complete your own copy of this diagram.

In each box, note a factor that made the Good Friday Agreement of 1998 possible. Add extra boxes if you need them. Colour code the finished diagram to show

a) the influence of individuals
b) developments outside Northern Ireland
c) developments inside Northern Ireland.

[ ] [ ] [ ]

Changes in attitude of Republic

[ ]

Contribution of President Clinton

[ ] [ ] Hume–Adams talks

2. Look at your factors again. Sort them into two categories:
a) essential factors (without these no agreement was possible)
b) significant factors (these helped achieve an agreement but it could have happened without them).

3. Decide whether each of your factors mostly
a) addressed a modern (post-1969) political issue
b) addressed a deep-rooted historical problem.

4. Finally, decide how far you agree with these statements:

■ 'History was never really the problem in Northern Ireland: it was politics. Two groups wanted power, and neither wanted to compromise. Then they went looking for suitable bits of history to use as an excuse.'

■ 'The Good Friday Agreement allowed Northern Ireland's people to rid themselves of the burden of history.'

Use your answers to prepare a presentation showing how effective you think the Good Friday Agreement was.

■ COURSEWORK ASSIGNMENT

'What made the Good Friday Agreement possible?'

Many factors made the Good Friday Agreement possible:

■ the contributions of important individuals
■ the importance of developments outside Northern Ireland
■ the actions of paramilitaries and their representatives
■ the part played by Northern Ireland's democratic political parties
■ the role of the British and Irish governments
■ the role played by ordinary people
■ the importance of previous developments in the 1970s, 1980s and 1990s.

The question is asking you to explain why something has happened. You know that the causes were complicated and several were involved. These have been listed for you. But simply describing each of these in detail does not explain why the Agreement was made. Nor does describing everything that has happened in Northern Ireland in the last 30 years. To tackle this assignment you should:

1. Choose factors which you think made the Good Friday Agreement possible.
2. Explain how each of the factors contributed.
3. Show how they were linked to each other. You could mention how they were linked to some other factors.
4. Finally, look at the examiner's' mark-scheme (you can get this from your teacher) to check what they are looking for.

LOOKING FORWARD: PEACE AT LAST?

Did the Good Friday Agreement mean that Northern Ireland's troubles were over?

SOURCE 1 From the *Sunday Mirror*, 14 May 1998

A VOTE FOR PEACE

OUR GREAT DAY

Northern Ireland turns its back on the bombs and bullets

YES   VOT RECO

JUBILANT: SDLP's John Hume, left, and Unionist David Trimble

Optimism versus pessimism

When the first newspapers emerged after the Good Friday Agreement, the tone was one of cautious celebration.

When the people of Ireland, North and South, voted 'Yes' in the referendum of May 1998, it really did seem like the time to celebrate. However, there were many people, especially in Northern Ireland, who were still concerned. In the months after the Agreement, there were probably many conversations like these going on.

The Northern Ireland Assembly

The Assembly has made good progress. It first met on 1 July 1998. It appointed the well-respected Lord Alderdice as its Speaker, David Trimble as First Minister and the SDLP's Seamus Mallon as his deputy. Northern Ireland politicians were in the same building, and arguing like normal politicians!

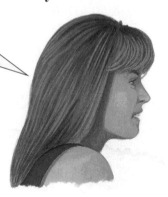

Yes, it did make a good start. But by 1999, the Assembly had not appointed a cabinet. The process was completely hung up on the lack of progress made in decommissioning IRA weapons. In July 1999 the Assembly fell apart when Unionists refused to take part in forming a new government because the IRA had not started decommissioning weapons. Senator George Mitchell had to be called back to carry out a review to rescue the whole peace process.

Paramilitaries

> In the next few years, we should see an end to political violence altogether. It must be hard for victims' families to watch prisoners being released early, but without releases it is hard to see how peace will last.

> But there has been no decommissioning of any weapons. Also, paramilitary punishment beatings of people in their own areas have not stopped. What's more, the release of paramilitary prisoners is an insult to the families and loved ones of thousands of innocent victims.

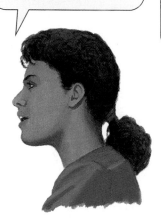

Security and policing

> It might be said that in 1969 the RUC and B-Specials were not always impartial. Today's RUC is professional and well disciplined. It stood up to the Loyalists at Drumcree in 1998 and 1999. The independent commission set up by the government has already heard from 9000 people. When it reports in 2000, it will be clear that the RUC can win the confidence of both communities.

> Drumcree has helped, but many Nationalists still don't trust the RUC. They remember internment and allegations of human rights abuses. They want the RUC disbanded and they won't accept anything less. Even moderate Catholics or Nationalists are reluctant to join the RUC because republican activists harass and intimidate their families.

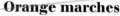

The republican movement

> Gerry Adams has won over most Republicans to a non-violent approach. The Omagh bomb of August 1998 was horrific and inexcusable, but it might be a turning point. All Nationalists were appalled by this vicious slaughter. In the Republic, where the alleged killers were based, people were horrified. After the Omagh bomb, there is not one shred of sympathy left for violent republicanism. That means republican extremists have nowhere to hide. Their time is over.

> There are still plenty of hardliners in the republican movement who will never accept anything but a 32-county Irish Republic. Also, public opinion in the Republic was appalled by the Enniskillen bombing in 1987 but the men and women of violence still found somewhere to hide. These extremists really believe they are right, so they'll be back.

Orange marches

> OK, I accept that the violent clashes at Drumcree have not reflected much credit on anyone. The Orangemen insist on marching down the mainly Catholic Garvaghy Road (which was once mainly Protestant). The local residents' groups don't want them to. But Drumcree's an extreme example. There are thousands of peaceful Orange marches every summer in Northern Ireland, and only about 50 are disputed. In July 1998, the Orange Order called off another of the big controversial marches, on the Ormeau Road, in Belfast.

> Drumcree has shown there is a core of loyalist hardliners associated with the Orange Order. They killed an RUC officer in riots at Drumcree in July 1998. In December 1998, they brought Portadown to a halt with a demonstration about the Drumcree march (Drumcree is on the edge of Portadown). Local traders were furious at losing their Christmas trade.

What does the evidence suggest?

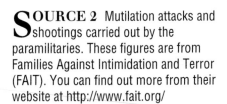

SOURCE 2 Mutilation attacks and shootings carried out by the paramilitaries. These figures are from Families Against Intimidation and Terror (FAIT). You can find out more from their website at http://www.fait.org/

SOURCE 3 Philip Dean, a member of the Ulster Democratic Party, one of the smaller unionist parties, commenting on prisoner releases in an e-mail conference in May 1998

66 Prisoner release has played a part in conflict resolution throughout the world. Those who have been part of the problem must be part of the solution. But only those who are committed to purely peaceful and democratic means and those whose parent organisation is on ceasefire. No ceasefire, no release! 99

SOURCE 4 A poster published by hardline Republicans attacking the Good Friday Agreement, 1998. The poster shows Mo Mowlam, Gerry Adams and Martin McGuinness. 'Gerry and the Peacemakers' is a pun on the 1960s pop band Gerry and the Pacemakers. The sell-out tour is an ironic reference to this 'band' who have not sold out their tour in terms of tickets, but have allegedly sold out their supporters and friends

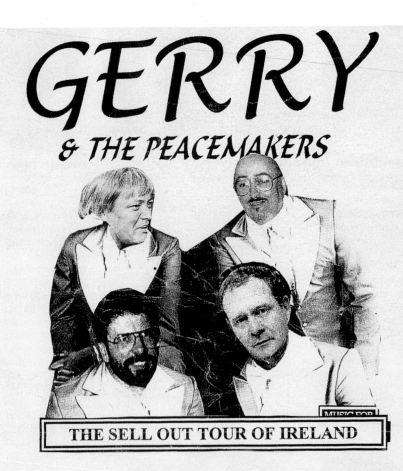

GERRY & THE PEACEMAKERS

THE SELL OUT TOUR OF IRELAND

PRISONERS - *SOLD OUT*

REPUBLICAN IDEALS - *SOLD OUT*

ABSTENTIONISM - *SOLD OUT*

STORMONT TALKS - *SOLD OUT*

DOWNING STREET VISIT - *SOLD OUT*

A 32 COUNTY IRELAND - *SOLD OUT*

SOURCE 6 Part of a statement by Brian O'Neill, August 1998. O'Neill was a leader of a demonstration in Dundalk, in the Irish Republic, held to protest about the Omagh bombing. Dundalk was a traditional republican stronghold, and home of the 32-County Sovereignty Committee. This was said to be the political wing of the Real IRA. Two Spanish students were killed in the explosion at Omagh. They were on an exchange with Irish students

66 *We want to express revulsion at the atrocity in Omagh; and express community sympathy with the families who lost loved ones and the injured of Omagh, Buncrana and the Spanish student group.*

We also want to express solidarity with the peace process and re-affirm the referendum vote in favour of the Good Friday Agreement. We will demonstrate our disgust at those who without any mandate are bringing disgrace to the town of Dundalk.

We are saying directly to the 32-County Movement and the 'Real IRA' that there will be no hiding place in Dundalk or County Louth for their activities, and that the people of Dundalk and Louth support the government, the Gardai [the Irish police] and the RUC to take whatever action is necessary to crush the activities of those organisations still involved in violence and terror. 99

SOURCE 5 A still from video footage showing the devastation in the centre of Omagh, County Tyrone, in August 1998. A breakaway republican group called the Real IRA exploded a car bomb outside a children's clothes shop. An incorrect warning meant people were gathered near the bomb. The final death toll was 29

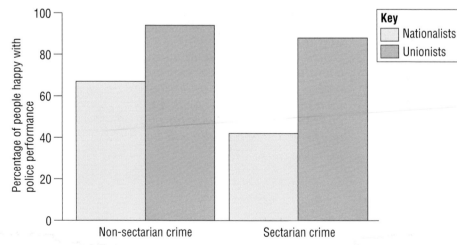

SOURCE 7 The results of a study by the University of Ulster into attitudes towards the police, published in 1997

■ **TASK**

The conversations on pages 128–129 set out the pessimistic and optimistic views on

■ the Northern Ireland Assembly
■ paramilitaries
■ the republican movement
■ security and policing
■ Orange marches

1. Work in groups of five, and take one issue each.
2. For your issue, decide whether you would side with the optimists or the pessimists. Make sure you can explain and support your view. Use Sources 2–7 to help you. You may want to use the internet or other resources for extra research. Your teacher may be able to suggest some useful websites.

Predictions: what does the future hold?

■ SOURCE INVESTIGATION

A book like this is always impossible to finish. Once it has been written, it has to be set out, checked, printed and so on. In the time that this takes, Northern Ireland has moved on again! So here are the best guesses of some people who know about Northern Ireland on the developments and issues facing the province following the Good Friday Agreement.

SOURCE 8 Rev. John Dunlop, Minister of Rosemary Presbyterian Church, Belfast

66 *The Good Friday Agreement of 1998 represents an attempt to overcome the politics of 'control and exclusion' by substituting in its place the politics of 'co-operation and inclusion'.*

The Agreement was reached in an Ireland which is changing rapidly. The people of the Republic of Ireland, with a youthful population, have found a confidence within the European Union which has diminished anti-British sentiments, and the Second Vatican Council [of the Catholic Church] has opened up new relationships between the Churches. In historical terms, this is new. We have not been here before. This will, I believe, continue to develop.

It is likely that identity definition, which has been forged in opposition to one's enemies, will diminish through the experience of co-operation. This should lead to a greater appreciation of diversity. As political responsibility is also devolved in Scotland and Wales, there will be new debates about what it is to be English and British. People will ask how racial minorities fit into the definition of being English.

Since ministers in the Northern Ireland Executive will hold positions by right of electoral party strength, one of the difficulties which we may face in the future is how the electorate can dismiss members of the Executive if they prove to be incompetent. 99

SOURCE 9 Michael Hall, a community activist who works with both the Catholic and Protestant communities in Belfast. Michael publishes a series of pamphlets on the lives, views and attitudes of people in Belfast. They are called Island pamphlets

66 *Throughout the horrors of the Troubles, one of the few positive developments has been the remarkable blossoming of community action. To me, it was the constant pressure from the grass roots which provided the real driving force which pushed this society, and its politicians, into grasping the current possibilities for peace. Admittedly, those politicians are presently baulking [hesitating] at the latest hurdles, but hopefully these will be overcome, for few in this society desire a return to violence. And yet, ironically, as a genuine peace is gradually forged, my fear is that community activists will be inexorably [inevitably] pushed to the side.*

Some politicians are already intimating [hinting] that they want the community sector to assume a subservient [inferior] position and cease intruding upon their 'territory'. If our communities prove unable to prevent this, I fear that the obstacles still ahead will threaten a return to confrontational politics. But if our communities can resist, and manage to find outlets whereby their collective voice can be heard, then in that voice will lie this society's only real guarantee that the peace for which we have worked so determinedly will not be prematurely snatched away. 99

SOURCE 10 Sheelagh Dean, Vivien Kelly and Heather Thompson, history teachers and advisers in Northern Ireland

66 *After ten years of peace, Northern Ireland will be an exciting place to live, with a vibrant economy. It will be an integral part of Europe and people will think of themselves as European as much as British or Irish. Cross-border co-operation will be more routine, and the world media's interest in the political situation in Northern Ireland will have declined, to be replaced by a more positive image. Northern Ireland's highly educated workforce will be utilised within the country because of increased opportunities offered by technology, tourism and service industries. More people will vote on social and economic issues rather than along sectarian lines.* 99

SOURCE 11 Dr Roger Austin, lecturer at the University of Ulster, Coleraine

66 *One of the key issues arising from the 1998 Agreement will be the extent to which violence continues to diminish as a feature of life in Northern Ireland. My own hunch is that there will be occasional and localised outbursts from paramilitaries, but there will be nothing like the scale of violence involving the army, police, paramilitaries and members of the public.*

This will have huge consequences, because it will allow natural cross-community contact within Northern Ireland to develop and this in turn will help to build trust between people who often hold unfounded and negative views of 'the other side'.

This process will not be confined to Northern Ireland but will extend to cross-border links between Northern Ireland and the Republic of Ireland, based on commerce and sectors of the public service, including education. This will help to promote understanding between cultures and lead to areas of mutual co-operation between Belfast and Dublin where it is in the interests of both sides that this should happen. At the same time, it seems likely that the dominant position of the Churches in the lives of people on both sides of the border will gradually decline, as it has done in other western European countries. Alongside these two factors, it seems probable that a period of peace will encourage business investment from both the European Union and the USA, and this will help to reduce the economic problems that played a part in the Troubles.

Britain's special interest in Northern Ireland is also likely to weaken once peace and stable political structures are in place and shown to be working. This will happen partly because more decisions affecting the lives of people are taken by the Council of Ministers in Brussels, and also by the general trend to devolving local powers to regional assemblies. The upshot of all these trends over the next twenty years will be for people in Northern Ireland to move closer to their neighbours in the Republic of Ireland, but without any concerted pressure for a political uniting of the two parts of the island. 99

1. Decide whether each of the predictors in this section is an optimist or a pessimist and in what areas.
2. Evaluate the views of the people in Sources 8–11 in the light of events and developments since these predictions were written in early 1999.

a) What have the people been right about so far?
b) What have they been wrong about so far?
c) What is it too early to judge on?
   You should have plenty of up-to-date information of your own but pages 134–135 give a quick overview of some of the most recent happenings.

Events and developments

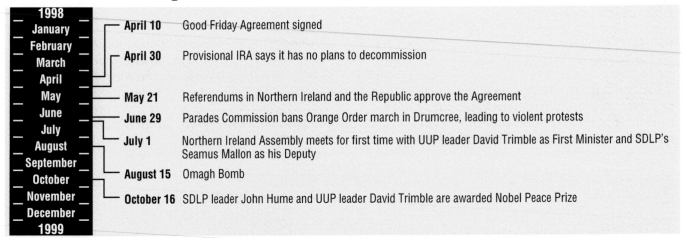

1998		
April 10	Good Friday Agreement signed
April 30	Provisional IRA says it has no plans to decommission
May 21	Referendums in Northern Ireland and the Republic approve the Agreement
June 29	Parades Commission bans Orange Order march in Drumcree, leading to violent protests
July 1	Northern Ireland Assembly meets for first time with UUP leader David Trimble as First Minister and SDLP's Seamus Mallon as his Deputy
August 15	Omagh Bomb
October 16	SDLP leader John Hume and UUP leader David Trimble are awarded Nobel Peace Prize

1998 January February March April May June July August September October November December 1999

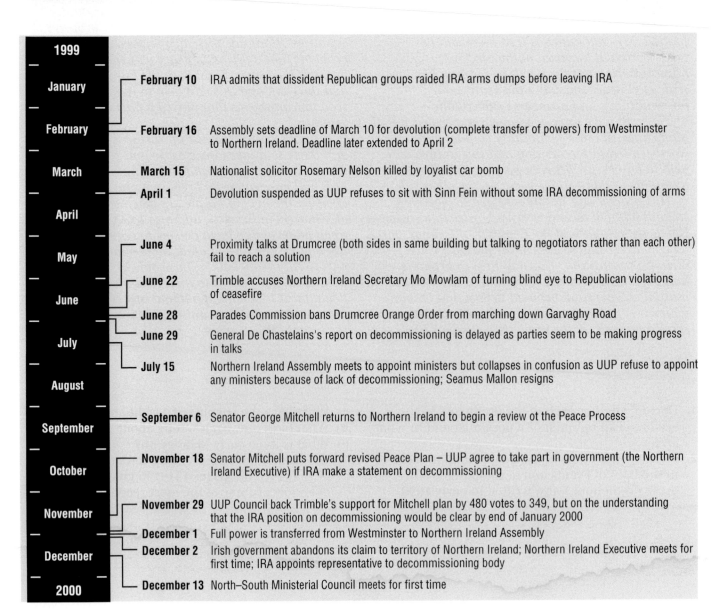

1999		
February 10	IRA admits that dissident Republican groups raided IRA arms dumps before leaving IRA
February 16	Assembly sets deadline of March 10 for devolution (complete transfer of powers) from Westminster to Northern Ireland. Deadline later extended to April 2
March 15	Nationalist solicitor Rosemary Nelson killed by loyalist car bomb
April 1	Devolution suspended as UUP refuses to sit with Sinn Fein without some IRA decommissioning of arms
June 4	Proximity talks at Drumcree (both sides in same building but talking to negotiators rather than each other) fail to reach a solution
June 22	Trimble accuses Northern Ireland Secretary Mo Mowlam of turning blind eye to Republican violations of ceasefire
June 28	Parades Commission bans Drumcree Orange Order from marching down Garvaghy Road
June 29	General De Chastelains's report on decommissioning is delayed as parties seem to be making progress in talks
July 15	Northern Ireland Assembly meets to appoint ministers but collapses in confusion as UUP refuse to appoint any ministers because of lack of decommissioning; Seamus Mallon resigns
September 6	Senator George Mitchell returns to Northern Ireland to begin a review ot the Peace Process
November 18	Senator Mitchell puts forward revised Peace Plan – UUP agree to take part in government (the Northern Ireland Executive) if IRA make a statement on decommissioning
November 29	UUP Council back Trimble's support for Mitchell plan by 480 votes to 349, but on the understanding that the IRA position on decommissioning would be clear by end of January 2000
December 1	Full power is transferred from Westminster to Northern Ireland Assembly
December 2	Irish government abandons its claim to territory of Northern Ireland; Northern Ireland Executive meets for first time; IRA appoints representative to decommissioning body
December 13	North–South Ministerial Council meets for first time

1999 January February March April May June July August September October November December 2000

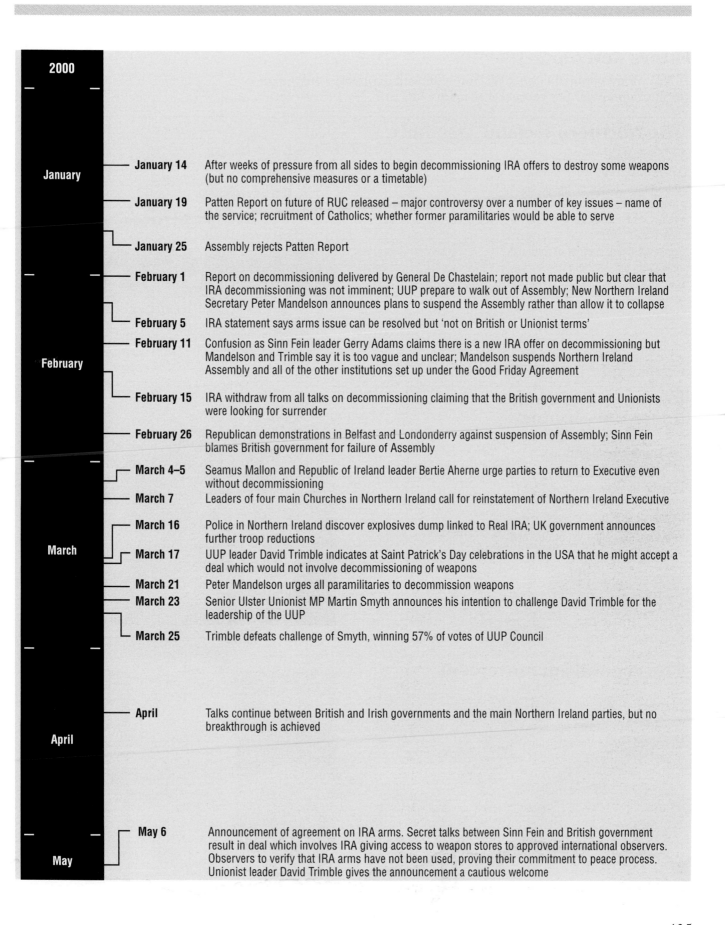

2000

January

January 14   After weeks of pressure from all sides to begin decommissioning IRA offers to destroy some weapons (but no comprehensive measures or a timetable)

January 19   Patten Report on future of RUC released – major controversy over a number of key issues – name of the service; recruitment of Catholics; whether former paramilitaries would be able to serve

January 25   Assembly rejects Patten Report

February 1   Report on decommissioning delivered by General De Chastelain; report not made public but clear that IRA decommissioning was not imminent; UUP prepare to walk out of Assembly; New Northern Ireland Secretary Peter Mandelson announces plans to suspend the Assembly rather than allow it to collapse

February 5   IRA statement says arms issue can be resolved but 'not on British or Unionist terms'

February 11   Confusion as Sinn Fein leader Gerry Adams claims there is a new IRA offer on decommissioning but Mandelson and Trimble say it is too vague and unclear; Mandelson suspends Northern Ireland Assembly and all of the other institutions set up under the Good Friday Agreement

February

February 15   IRA withdraw from all talks on decommissioning claiming that the British government and Unionists were looking for surrender

February 26   Republican demonstrations in Belfast and Londonderry against suspension of Assembly; Sinn Fein blames British government for failure of Assembly

March 4–5   Seamus Mallon and Republic of Ireland leader Bertie Aherne urge parties to return to Executive even without decommissioning

March 7   Leaders of four main Churches in Northern Ireland call for reinstatement of Northern Ireland Executive

March 16   Police in Northern Ireland discover explosives dump linked to Real IRA; UK government announces further troop reductions

March

March 17   UUP leader David Trimble indicates at Saint Patrick's Day celebrations in the USA that he might accept a deal which would not involve decommissioning of weapons

March 21   Peter Mandelson urges all paramilitaries to decommission weapons

March 23   Senior Ulster Unionist MP Martin Smyth announces his intention to challenge David Trimble for the leadership of the UUP

March 25   Trimble defeats challenge of Smyth, winning 57% of votes of UUP Council

April   Talks continue between British and Irish governments and the main Northern Ireland parties, but no breakthrough is achieved

April

May 6   Announcement of agreement on IRA arms. Secret talks between Sinn Fein and British government result in deal which involves IRA giving access to weapon stores to approved international observers. Observers to verify that IRA arms have not been used, proving their commitment to peace process. Unionist leader David Trimble gives the announcement a cautious welcome

May

Future developments

This book was published in 2000. You will need to update yourself on key developments. You can use a structure like this.

The Northern Ireland Assembly

Key developments (with dates)	
Importance (based on points like the amount of media coverage, the impact on the peace process or on ordinary people)	
Supports the pessimist or optimist view (with explanation)	

Paramilitaries and decommissioning

Key developments (with dates)	
Importance (based on points like the amount of media coverage, the impact on the peace process or on ordinary people)	
Supports the pessimist or optimist view (with explanation)	

The republican movement

Key developments (with dates)	
Importance (based on points like the amount of media coverage, the impact on the peace process or on ordinary people)	
Supports the pessimist or optimist view (with explanation)	

Security and policing

Key developments (with dates)	
Importance (based on points like the amount of media coverage, the impact on the peace process or on ordinary people)	
Supports the pessimist or optimist view (with explanation)	

Orange marches

Key developments (with dates)	
Importance (based on points like the amount of media coverage, the impact on the peace process or on ordinary people)	
Supports the pessimist or optimist view (with explanation)	

Glossary

ANGLICAN one of the Protestant churches in Ireland, the church of Ireland

BLACK AND TANS special force created by British Prime Minister David Lloyd George in 1920 to help fight the IRA

B-SPECIALS part time armed Special Police Constables who served in Northern Ireland from 1922 until 1970

BY ELECTION one-off election held between major elections, usually because of the death or resignation of an MP or councillor

CELT /CELTIC ancient peoples who migrated to Ireland and settled it in the Iron Age

CIVIL RIGHTS equal treatment for all citizens, whatever their religion, nationality or political beliefs

COMMISSION an investigation into particular events, usually set up by the government and headed by a senior judge

CONSTITUTION the basic rules which set out how a country is run and how it makes its laws

CURFEW a restriction placed on people in a certain place, usually preventing them from going out of their homes after dark

DAIL EIREANN the parliament of the Republic of Ireland, set up in 1918 when Ireland was still ruled by Britain

DECOMMISSIONING process in which paramilitary groups in Northern Ireland give up their weapons

DUP Democratic Unionist Party, hard line Loyalist party led by Ian Paisley

EASTER RISING rebellion against British rule organised by the Irish Republican Brotherhood which took place on Easter Monday 1916

ECUMENICAL a movement which involved different Churches communicating and co-operating with each other

FENIANS name often given to the Irish Republican Brotherhood. Fenians were originally an invincible army from ancient Irish mythology

GAELIC term to describe ancient Irish language, culture and people

GERRYMANDERING arranging the boundaries of electoral districts in such a way as to distort the vote

GUERRILLA type of warfare involving hit and run attacks rather than open battles

HOME RULE measure to give Ireland its own parliament to rule itself, but leaving Ireland within the British empire

HUMANITARIAN concern for human dignity and compassion

INLA Irish National Liberation Army, a Republican paramilitary group formed in 1974

INTEGRATED schools which educate students from all communities in Northern Ireland rather than Protestant or Catholic

INTERNMENT policy of arresting and holding suspects without trial

IRA Irish Republican Army – republican paramilitary organisation formed in 1919 and active at various stages of the conflict in Northern Ireland

IRB Irish Republican Brotherhood – republican organisation, also known as Fenians, formed in 1858

JACOBITE supporters of Catholic King James II in the late 1600s

LOYALISM /LOYALIST hardline Unionism – loyalists are loyal to the monarch of the United Kingdom

LOYAL ORANGE ORDER a Protestant organisation formed in 1795 – opposed to the Catholic Church, connected to unionist political parties and best known for marches and parades

NATIONALISM /NATIONALIST political view which wants a united Ireland free of connections to the United Kingdom

OMBUDSMAN a government official whose role is to investigate complaints into the actions of local councils or similar organisations

PARAMILITARIES violent republican and loyalist organisations

POLITICAL PRISONER person in prison because of political beliefs rather than having committed any crimes

PRESBYTERIAN one of the main Protestant churches in Northern Ireland

PROPORTIONAL REPRESENTATION system of voting which ensures minority groups gain fair representation in parliament

REFERENDUM vote on a key issue to see whether the population approves or disapproves of a particular action by the government

REPRISALS   revenge attacks

REPUBLICAN   extreme nationalist political view, usually prepared to support force to achieve a united Ireland with no connection to Britain

RUC   Royal Ulster Constabulary – police force of Northern Ireland

SDLP   Social and Democratic Labour Party – main democratic nationalist party in Northern Ireland

SECTARIAN   term used to describe religious and/or political conflict in Northern Ireland

SEGREGATED   separate schooling for Catholics and Protestants

SINN FEIN   republican political party with close links to the IRA

SOCIALISM   political belief which focuses on working people and poorer members of society to improve their lives by spreading wealth more evenly through society

STATUS QUO   the existing situation

TAOISEACH   leader of the Irish Republic (term first used by Eamon de Valera in 1937)

TROUBLES   conflict in Northern Ireland, can describe conflict of 1919–21 or from 1969 onwards

UDA   Ulster Defence Association – main loyalist paramilitary organisation

UFF   Ulster Freedom Fighters – loyalist paramilitary organisation

ULSTER   one of the four provinces which make up Ireland, consisting of nine counties

ULSTER UNIONIST PARTY   main Unionist party in Northern Ireland

UNIONIST   political view supporting the parliamentary union of Great Britain and Northern Ireland

UNITED IRISHMEN   radical political movement which tried to break the links between Britain and Ireland in the 1790s

UVF   Ulster Volunteer Force – loyalist paramilitary organisation

Index

Source acknowledgements

The Publishers would like to thank the following for permission to reproduce copyright material:

Photographs:
p.3 *t* courtesy the Northern Ireland Tourist Board, *b* Brian Aris/Camera Press; **p.4** Source, *Drawing Support 2: Murals of War and Peace*, Belfast, Beyond the Pale Publications 1995, p.34; **p.5** *tl* Pacemaker Press, *tr* Popperfoto/Reuters, *b* Belfast Telegraph Newspapers; **p.9** © Punch Ltd; **p.13** *t* courtesy Killaloo True Blues, *b* Northern Ireland Political Collection, Linen Hall Library, Belfast; **p.14** Source, *Drawing Support 2: Murals of War and Peace*, Belfast, Beyond the Pale Publications 1995, p.17; **p.15** Source, *Drawing Support 2: Murals of War and Peace*, Belfast, Beyond the Pale Publications 1995, p.17; **p.17** *t* The British Library, *c* Public Record Office of Northern Ireland, *b* The British Library (Add. 72869, fols 86v &88); **p.18** Fotomas Index; **p.20** *t* Source, *Drawing Support: Murals in the North of Ireland*, Belfast, Beyond the Pale Publications 1992, p.1, *b* Northern Ireland Political Collection, Linen Hall Library, Belfast; **p.22** Source, *Drawing Support: Murals in the North of Ireland*, Belfast, Beyond the Pale Publications 1992, p.1; **p.24** *tr* Northern Ireland Political Collection, Linen Hall Library, Belfast/An Phoblacht, *l & br* Northern Ireland Political Collection, Linen Hall Library, Belfast; **p.27** National Museum of Ireland; **p.31** *t & b* National Museum of Ireland; **p.32** The Illustrated London News Picture Library; **p.33** *t* Hulton Getty, *bl & br* National Museum of Ireland; **p.34** © Punch Ltd; **p.38** *t* courtesy the Northern Ireland Tourist Board, *b* © National Museums & Galleries of Northern Ireland, Ulster Folk & Transport Museum (Neg. L4339-14); **p.39** *t* Northern Ireland Political Collection, Linen Hall Library, Belfast; **p.42** National Museum of Ireland; **p.44** National Musuem of Ireland; **p.46** Northern Ireland Political Collection, Linen Hall Library, Belfast; **p.50** Evening Standard; **p.51** *t* Hulton Getty, *c* Camera Press, *b* Topham Picturepoint; **p.54** *t & b* Hulton Getty; **p.55** Public Record Office of Northern Ireland; **p.60** Northern Ireland Political Collection, Linen Hall Library, Belfast; **p.61** Belfast Telegraph Newspapers; **p.63** *l* Hulton Getty, *r* Paul Schartzman/Camera Press; **p.64** Hulton Getty; **p.68** *t* Public Record Office of Northern Ireland, *b* Northern Ireland Political Collection, Linen Hall Library, Belfast; **p.69** *tl* Colman Doyle/Camera Press, *tr* Camera Press, *b* Hulton Getty; **p.70** PA News Photo Library; **p.71** Popperfoto; **p.72** Belfast Telegraph Newspapers; **p.74** *t* Northern Ireland Political Collection, Linen Hall Library, Belfast, *b* © Kelvin Boyes; **p.77** photograph copyright Barney McMonagle/Guildhall Press; **p.79** *tl & bl* photograph copyright Barney McMonagle/Guildhall Press, *tr* Popperfoto, *br* Michael McQueen/Camera Press; **p.80** Camera Press; **p.81** Belfast Telegraph Newspapers; **p.83** Colman Doyle/Camera Press; **p.87** *t* Source, *Drawing Support: Murals in the North of Ireland*, Belfast, Beyond the Pale Publications 1992, p.42, *b* Victor Patterson/Camera Press; **p.90** *t* Mark Fenn/Camera Press, *b* Pacemaker Press; **p.92** Pacemaker Press; **p.93** Source, *Drawing Support 2: Murals of War and Peace*, Belfast, Beyond the Pale Publications 1995, p.24; **p.94** © John Kent/Times Newspapers Limited, 17th April 1999; **p.96** Colman Doyle/Camera Press; **p.98** © Cormac; **p.99** Popperfoto; **p.100** Source, *Drawing Support: Murals in the North of Ireland*, Belfast, Beyond the Pale Publications 1992, p.42; **p.101** Northern Ireland Political Collection, Linen Hall Library, Belfast/An Phoblacht; **p.103** © Trog/The Observer, 25 November 1973; **p.104** Victor Patterson/Camera Press; **p.105** © Fortnight/Blotski; **p.106** PA News Photo Library/Stefan Rousseau; **p.109** *t* Martyn Turner/The Irish Times, *b* The Irish Times; **p.111** Pacemaker Press; **p.112** Popperfoto/Reuters; **p.113** Pacemaker Press; **p.114** © Steve Bell. All rights reserved.; **p.115** Martyn Turner/The Irish Times; **p.116** *t* Evening Standard, *b* Martyn Turner/The Irish Times; **p.117** Northern Ireland Political Collection, Linen Hall Library, Belfast; **p.118** Popperfoto/Reuters; **p.119** *tl* Northern Ireland Political Collection, Linen Hall Library, Belfast/NUS-USI, *tr* Pacemaker Press, *b* courtesy Lagan College, Belfast; **p.120** Martyn Turner/The Irish Times; **p.121** *l & r* reproduced courtesy of The Warrington Project; **p.123** PA News Photo Library; **p.122** *t* Source, *Drawing Support: Murals in the North of Ireland*, Belfast, Beyond the Pale Publications 1992, p.49, *b* Northern Ireland Political Collection, Linen Hall Library, Belfast/An Phoblacht; **p.124** PA News Photo Library/Martin McCullough; **p.125** Popperfoto/Reuters; **p.126** The Irish Times; **p.127** *t* Popperfoto/Reuters, *b* © Joanne O'Brien/Format; **p.128** headline © Sunday Mirror; **p.130** Northern Ireland Political Collection, Linen Hall Library, Belfast; **p.131** Pacemaker Press.

Written sources:
p.19 Extract from *Young Ned of the Hill*, The Pogues, Perfect Songs Ltd, Proper Music Publishing Ltd; **p.58** Ciaran McKeown, *The Passion of Peace*, The Blackstaff Press, 1984; **p.75 & p.78** Raymond McClean, *The Road to Bloody Sunday*, The Guildhall Press, 1983 (revised 1997); **p.120** Martyn Turner, *Pack Up Your Troubles – 25 Years of Northern Ireland Cartoons*, Blackstaff Press, 1995.

Every effort has been made to trace all copyright holders, but if any have been inadvertently overlooked the Publishers will be pleased to make the necessary arrangements at the first opportunity.